Dr. Brooks Preacher

ACADEMIC TURMOIL

Books by Theodore L. Gross

ALBION W. TOURGÉE (1963)
THOMAS NELSON PAGE (1967)
HAWTHORNE, MELVILLE, STEPHEN CRANE:
A CRITICAL BIBLIOGRAPHY (1971)
(with Stanley Wertheim)
THE HEROIC IDEAL IN AMERICAN LITERATURE (1971)
ACADEMIC TURMOIL (1980)

EDITOR

FICTION (1967)
(with Norman Kelvin)
DARK SYMPHONY: NEGRO LITERATURE IN AMERICA (1968)
(with James Emanuel)
REPRESENTATIVE MEN: CULT HEROES OF
OUR TIME (1970)
A NATION OF NATIONS: ETHNIC LITERATURE
IN AMERICA (1971)
THE LITERATURE OF AMERICAN JEWS (1973)
AMERICA IN LITERATURE (1978)
(General Editor)

ACADEMIC TURMOIL

The Reality and Promise of Open Education

THEODORE L. GROSS

Anchor Press/Doubleday
GARDEN CITY, NEW YORK
1980

Portions of this book originally appeared in *Saturday Review,* February 4, 1978, and in *Change,* June–July 1978

ISBN: 0-385-14904-2
Library of Congress Catalog Card Number 79-7674

For Selma

CONTENTS

. . . for we must consider that we shall be as a city upon a hill, the eyes of all people are upon us . . .

John Winthrop
First Governor, Massachusetts Bay Company
A Model of Christian Charity, 1630
(Written on board the *Arbella,*
on the Atlantic Ocean)

The experiment is to be tried, whether the highest education can be given to the masses, whether the children of the people—the children of the whole people—can be educated; and whether an institution of learning of the highest grade can be successfully controlled by the popular will, not by the privileged few.

Horace Webster
President
The Free Academy (later to be named
The College of the City of New York), 1847

A democracy is more than a form of government; it is primarily a mode of associated living, of conjoint communicated experience. The extension into space of the number of individuals who participate in an interest so that each has to refer his own action to that of others, and to consider the action of others to give point and direction to his own, is equivalent to the breaking down of those barriers of class, race, and national territory which kept men from perceiving the full import of their activity. These more numerous and more varied points of contact denote a greater diversity of stimuli to which an individual has to respond; they consequently put a premium on variation in his action. They secure a liberation of powers which remain suppressed as long as the incitations to actions are partial, as they must be in a group which in its exclusiveness shuts out many interests.

John Dewey
Democracy and Education, 1916

ACADEMIC TURMOIL

ONE

Open Admissions: A Personal Account

I

For six years, from 1972 until 1978, my office was on the ground floor of Lincoln Corridor in an old Gothic building called Shepard Hall at The City College of New York, 138th Street and Convent Avenue, Harlem. Outside this office, on makeshift benches, students used to congregate—black, Puerto Rican, Asian, and varieties of ethnic white—studying texts, preparing papers, playing the radio, moving back and forth to classes, lingering in a space that had come to serve as a temporary lounge—a passageway that led from the campus to the classrooms to a terrace looking eastward over Harlem.

As Dean of Humanities, I moved among these students and conducted my business in adjacent rooms which featured telephones and filing cabinets, typewriters, a copying machine, a dictaphone, and a wall of books that, from the point of view of European culture, represented the best that had been thought and said.

As an administrator, I was responsible for the study of humanities: foreign languages, English and speech, music, art, drama, and, because of circumstances special to this urban college, Asian and Jewish Studies. The two other ethnic studies departments—Black and Puerto Rican Studies—reported to the Dean of Social Science, who lived on the other side of Lincoln Corridor. Twenty thousand students, day and evening, were enrolled in courses—to speak only of the humanities—ranging from Shakespeare to Ray Bradbury, from Beethoven to Charlie Parker, from W. E. B. Du Bois to Richard Wright, from Confucius and Martin Buber to Mao and Philip Roth, from Basic Writing 1 for the poorly prepared to Creative Writing taught by the most sophisticated American novelists. By 1974 the student population was multi-ethnic: 31 per cent black, 15 per cent Spanish, 6 per cent Asian, and diminishing percentages of Italians, Irish, Ukrainians, and Slavs—a microcosm, as we proudly used to say, of the world.

It was not always so. In the sixties, the college had been almost entirely white, with very little connection to the black, Puerto Rican, or Asian communities in New York—an urban college with a conventional curriculum and special programs for foreigners who had experienced problems with the English language. From one point of view, the college had been loyal to its legacy—admissions were only open to those who qualified through high school averages—and it had remained "an institution of learning of the highest grade." From another perspective, it had not been "controlled by the popular will"—not when scarcely 5 per cent of the entering students who qualified for admission were black and Puerto Rican in a city whose minorities (by 1970) numbered more than 30 per cent of the total population of New York City. The college could have continued to be exclusive and insisted upon maintaining "academic standards," but it was clear that corrosive social problems—racism, poverty, fragmented family life—had created unacceptable conditions in education for the minority children of New York. The college that called itself "The City College of New York" had to respond to the poor preparation of high school graduates if it was not to repudiate its deeper legacy of educating "the children of the whole people."

In 1965, a pre-baccalaureate program called SEEK[1] was established to "redress the imbalance that presently exists in our educational system and to provide an opportunity for upward mobility to blacks, Puerto Ricans and other disadvantaged groups through higher education." It offered intensive counseling, financial aid, tutorial assistance, and special courses that integrated basic skills and subject matter. By 1972, 2,000 students—in a total college population of 20,000—were enrolled in SEEK and within the two-year period, from 1970–72, approximately 150 students were granted B.A. degrees. But in the sixties, the SEEK program had developed slowly and was peripheral to the activities of the college. No full commitment had yet been made to meet the needs of the rapidly growing black and Puerto Rican population in the city school system.

[1] Search for Education, Elevation, and Knowledge.

Within the college itself, the faculty had abolished requirements and prerequisites and had arranged elective courses in a cafeteria-style curriculum that made basic skills and basic knowledge seem irrelevant, structure obsolete, and sequential study unimportant. It was as if the college would now be attracting students so extremely well prepared that a laissez-faire approach to education could be tolerated: at the moment when standards had to be perpetuated, they were relaxed. The historical perspective was already suspect so that the liberal arts college functioned primarily on the pleasure principle. Students enrolled in the courses they wished. Economic growth was everywhere, and the college could afford small classes, independent study, and esoteric subjects.

During that time, summer riots sometimes jolted the academic community and created fears in the minds of those who sent their children to the campus on St. Nicholas Heights. At other times, assassinations like those of Malcolm X and Martin Luther King, and local uprisings, led by Stokely Carmichael and H. Rap Brown, sent terror through the college campus. These disturbances soon flared more frequently and burned closer to the campus. By 1969, flames were in our buildings. Decent human beings wrangled with one another: blacks confronted Jews, liberals shouted at conservatives, the young grumbled at their seniors, swingers taunted the sedate, women warned male administrators, Asians and blacks and Puerto Ricans caucused against the so-called white imperialistic educators of The City College.

The riots of affluent students at Columbia University

(only twenty city streets downtown) seemed academic in comparison to the anger of poor minorities, but they as well as other disturbances across the country fed the fury of those who once had been excluded from The City College of New York. In the spring of 1969, these black and Puerto Rican students, led by militants in and out of the college, presented "non-negotiable" demands to the administration, insisting that black and Puerto Ricans be admitted in proportion to their numbers in New York City, that admission should be independent of grades, and that a separate School of Black and Puerto Rican Studies be established. When these demands were not accepted, the South Campus was occupied and the president resigned.

Politics dictated educational policy. Arguments that once had been contained within classrooms and dining rooms raged through loud-speakers on an open campus while television and newspapers and radio recorded the changing history of New York. Educators who had blessed student protégés in the names of Melville, Joyce, and Kafka were now asked by minorities to say no in thunder to a form of education that had been exclusive, intellectually elitist, unresponsive to colored Americans, unyielding in its demands for only—*only* academic excellence.

The demands of the minorities—white radicals as well as those representing the Third World—seemed ideologically sound and in the best tradition of liberalism: A public institution of higher learning should educate all of the citizenry. In a city school system of more than 60 per cent minority students, a city college must open wide its doors, find ways to educate "the children of the whole people," and break the cycle of poor academic preparation that leads to unemployment and poverty and crime. What group of self-pronounced liberals could refuse that opportunity?

But beyond the platitudes and posturing, what should that education be? And were we who had advanced degrees from Columbia and N.Y.U., who had been trained to preserve the best that has been thought and said —were we prepared to teach Shakespeare to a student who two years earlier had been struggling to compose coherent sentences? And were those faculty who had been graduated from The City College itself—undergraduates in the forties, fifties, and sixties—trapped in a reactionary parochialism that prevented them from sympathizing with students so different from themselves, and were they using academic standards as a mask for their own deepest fears and anxieties? But, in fairness, could the new student learn to read Shakespeare, even if we learned how to teach him to do so? Should he be taught Shakespeare at all? Or should he, if he must enter college, be given the liberation of literacy—itself enough to be learned in four brief years—and sent on his way to ply a trade, watch television in the evenings, and maybe read—if he should read at all—a pictorial newspaper? Did we have an obligation to educate everyone, even in a democracy, by means of a college?

We had no choice. The city's Board of Higher Education told us to implement an Open Admissions policy that would assure every high school student, regardless of his record, acceptance at a college of the City University. For guaranteed entrance to the senior colleges, the high school graduate had to have a scholastic average of 80 per cent or had to be ranked in the upper half of his class. But the allocation system depended upon the student's own selection of a college within the City University system, and when fewer well-prepared high school graduates made The City College their first choice—fundamentally because of its Harlem location—those with lower scores were admitted. We had planned to initiate this dramatic change in our admissions policy by 1975, but pressures from minorities and from some students and faculty could not be resisted, and Open Admissions began abruptly in June of 1970.

One wonders now whether the more deliberate plans —the establishment of pre-college skills centers devoted to the underprepared, for example—would have been implemented if these pressures had not been applied and whether there would have been a more sensible, gradual transition into Open Admissions. The history of American public education or of racial affairs would not suggest so—in any event, we had no choice. The rise of a black middle class in the city; the increased number of minority students in the schools; the mounting presence of the SEEK program; the racial turbulence of the sixties throughout the country; the political visibility of newly independent African nations—these forces as well as the radicalism of the time initiated Open Admissions.

The impact was particularly severe at The City College of New York, where academic achievement was like a code of honor which had never included considerations of class, race, religion, or national origin. The City College had been the great tuition-free college whose diploma had had so special a meaning for alumni, the hard-earned diploma of the poor. The alumni were proud that they had been graduated; proud that they could claim as their classmates Jonas Salk and Alfred Kazin, Herman Badillo, Bernard Malamud, A. Philip Randolph, Arthur Kornberg, and A. M. Rosenthal; nostalgic about their youthful poverty and grateful to have escaped it through the college; strong-minded about their remembered hunger for learning and eager to preserve the meaning of that academic achievement.

Some of them were bitterly disaffected and renounced their alma mater because they believed it had betrayed the standards they had struggled to achieve. But most were bewildered by this new generation of students for whom the college had to "soften" those standards. These alumni distrusted the arguments about deprivation— hadn't they been deprived?—but they sensed that the quality of this current deprivation was different, linked to a racist society that they had disavowed; and even if it were not different, they could afford to be generous. Like many successful people, they wished to be tolerant and understanding, and they tried to fathom the meaning of Open Admissions as explained by the administrators of The City College, who struggled to maintain standards of excellence as they grappled with the overwhelming problems presented by the new students.

II

In May 1970, I was elected chairman of an English department composed of 125 full-time people and a range of part-time professors: visiting poets, novelists, and journalists. In June, the policy of Open Admissions at the City University was officially established. Although the enrollment of well-prepared students was not immediately affected—as late as 1972 the number of electives had not diminished significantly, and the best students were very good indeed—the addition of new learners who needed training in writing skills altered our personnel practices dramatically. By the end of August, I had hired twenty-one additional full-time faculty members, most of whom were candidates for the Ph.D. in New York universities, to teach what we called basic writing. Within a year, Open Admissions greatly modified our educational mission. A department that had offered 70 per cent of its courses in literature and the rest in some form of written composition now offered the reverse. We tried to hold on tenaciously to our elective courses—to protect our discipline—but with each semester they were less justified by enrollment figures, and after 1973 they began to decline sharply in number.

These basic writing courses were deeply remedial. The problem for one third of the students was literacy, for another third competence, for the last third college-level English. In addition, many more poorly prepared students of varied ethnic backgrounds—Asians, blacks, Hispanics, and white students—crowded the classrooms, bringing with them language and dialect problems that prevented them from understanding the most basic texts, face to face with a faculty that was intellectually unprepared and emotionally unwilling—liberals up against the wall. The faculty experienced a shock of cultural recognition, requiring rhetorical bridges which now seem even more rhetorical than they did in 1970. In a newsletter, distributed within the English department that year, I wrote:

> Many of us have been trained for an elitist profession, but we are asked to perform democratic tasks; we have written dissertations on Spenser, but we are teaching remedial writing; we are committed to the book, but the students have been culturally shaped by television and film; we have studied a body of culture that is fundamentally Anglo-Saxon, but we teach many students who are black and Asian and Spanish; we pay homage to the history of English literature, but we are surrounded by the consequences of American history and the political presence of America; we are in an "English" department, but our work is involved with the literature and with the language that is spoken by Americans.
>
> I list all of these paradoxes collectively because they form a background against which we seek to accomplish our central desire: the humanistic training of a new generation of students . . .

All true, I still believe, but the older professors who struggled to teach sentence fragments were scarcely appeased; they would not change. The younger faculty—those who had been hired in late August—were indeed writing dissertations on Spenser, and their graduate studies pulled them away from the hard reality of their teaching; they were academic schizophrenics, holding what seemed to be two opposing ideas—literacy and literature—in their minds at the same time.

Everywhere one turned were crowds; confusion; students lined up to register in the hallways of temporary facilities; others waiting for conferences outside little offices of English professors; still others crowded into the dining rooms and bookstores or packed into rented classroom space on Broadway and 134th Street, overlooking the roaring railroad tracks of the IRT.

The excessive numbers of poorly trained students, the inadequate physical conditions, and the weak preparation —if not outright resistance—of many faculty all strained the implementation of Open Admissions. For a college, after all, is like a home. Without a foundation, it crumbles. And unprepared students confronting unwilling faculty, when the numbers reach critical proportions, will dramatically affect the quality of education. When open revolt by a faculty does not occur, as in the sixties, then lethargy invades the spirit, as in the seventies, and they come not to care. Everyone begins to complain about facilities, pension benefits, the quality of lunchroom food, extraneous matters of the flesh; and the favorite subjects seem to be early retirement, fellowship leaves, released time from teaching.

Anyone who had ever passed through The City College knew that the physical conditions were as bad as those elsewhere in urban America. But once the student had entered the classroom, the peeling walls and encrusted windowpanes vanished—the electricity of mind compensated for everything. I remember having taught "Tintern Abbey" to the belching background music of a city bus, and it had worked. Now the students seemed so poorly prepared, one wondered how that poetry could survive in the classroom. Was all our time to be spent in shaping passable prose?

Into the midst of the radical change in the university came the union. Until 1970, the faculty had been represented by a "legislative conference," which waited until the New York City high school teachers had fought their way to a 5 or 10 per cent salary increase—and then received "parity" for its membership. That was really the extent of their unionization, and the chairperson of a department was scarcely affected. Chairpersons had been extraordinarily powerful in the days before Open Admissions, and one could trace the history of many academic departments—the quality of faculty appointments, the shape of the curriculum—through the long shadow of one individual, who usually remained in office for years. Some of these chairpersons had been extremely autocratic, and rumors involving bias toward religious groups or women in hiring and other personnel practices were not uncommon; to this extent the union was a significant expression of faculty rights and a curb on any individual's unilateral behavior. Some chairpersons—like those of the English department—had been remarkable leaders, combining a sensitivity to scholarship and a firm administrative hand, and had shaped extraordinary departments, leaving a legacy of excellence upon which the work of Open Admissions depended.

The college faculty elected to be represented by an affiliate of the American Federation of Teachers, a tough-minded union that secured in 1972 high salaries, lucrative fringe benefits, and a variety of other faculty "rights"—low workloads, sabbaticals, leaves, and protection against discrimination.

At one end of the age spectrum, the chairperson confronted tenure in the shape of senior professors who were sometimes slow to co-operate in the implementation of Open Admissions: they did not want to adapt to the new student body. At the other end, the union so protected non-tenured faculty that it was virtually impossible to dismiss them unless they were (to use the contractual word) "unsatisfactory." The chairperson was forced into an extremely formal response—what human being is absolutely "satisfactory" or "unsatisfactory" as a teacher?—that was inevitably unjust to the faculty member as well as to himself. One was cautious in expressing personal comments to the non-tenured, for they might be used in what were called "grievances"; indeed, official form letters soon had to be drafted by the central administration, checked by the lawyers who advised the Board of Higher Education, and given to deans and chairpersons so that they would not make any mistakes in an effort to humanize their letters of non-reappointment. The legalized bureaucracy of academic life had converted the profession into a job and the administration into an adversary: punch in, punch out; call in sick to take the day off; never remain a moment after hours without extra compensation. The unionized mentality reduced some teachers into people who often had no respect for their own work, although others —the majority, fortunately—found their professional dignity in performing the task at hand, whatever that teaching task might have been, however long it took. But in the process, which was aggravated by economic difficulties, the chairperson was reduced to being a manager and factotum. Authority was centralized in fewer and fewer people—the president, the provost, and, on occasion, a dean.

Everyone used the union, when it suited his purpose. This attitude was further exacerbated by the force of affirmative action, which made administrators extremely sensitive to the fair apportionment of positions or to decisions about non-reappointment. Minorities were underrepresented on the faculty, and one could scarcely contemplate dismissing a black, Puerto Rican, or woman unless that person were utterly incompetent. In one's mind was the constant tension between the indisputable need for more minorities on the faculty and the absence of a sizable pool of applicants (in the sciences) or the need not to yield standards too quickly to momentary demands. One knew that not only the union but also special interest groups, in and out of the university, would apply pressure: the Citizens Commission on Human Rights, a campus caucus, B'nai B'rith, the Sons of Italy, the NAACP, community organizations—the list seemed endless, and many of these groups tested the independence of administrators. Such conditions were not conducive to courage on the part of the faculty or to educational leadership and academic freedom; and the history of Open Admissions—from this angle of vision—is too often a history of political, economic, and moral compromise.

III

Open Admissions meant that blacks and Puerto Ricans and Asians studied at The City College in greater numbers for the first time. In the years from 1930–39, only 41 blacks had graduated from the college; from 1940–49, 113; from 1950–54, 165; and between 1954 and 1970, the numbers did not increase significantly. The direct reason for these appallingly low figures stemmed from the fact that approximately 5 per cent of the total number of students who qualified for entrance to The City College were black. Similar statistics can be furnished for the Puerto Rican population. In contrast, New York City's population by the mid-1960s was comprised of 17.3 per cent black, 11.2 per cent Puerto Rican—and by 1970 the shifts in demography brought the percentage of blacks to 20.3 and the Puerto Ricans to 10.3. In effect, Open Admissions gave minorities representation that was equal to their numbers in the city at large, although not to their numbers in the school system, which was already more than 60 per cent black and Puerto Rican.

It is important to note that black, Puerto Rican, and Asian students were by no means in the majority at The City College when Open Admissions began. In fact, more than 60 per cent of the student body was from poor white ethnic groups—Greeks, Italians, Irish, Jews, and others. Only 20.5 per cent were black, 6.6 per cent Puerto Rican, 5.2 per cent Asian.[2] Like the Irish, Italians, and Jews before them, they came from working class families who could scarcely afford to send their children to college— almost 80 per cent of the families had incomes of less than $16,000, 22 per cent less than $4,000; the median income ranged from $8,000 to $10,000. And like the majority of students everywhere in America—but especially among the working class—they regarded television and radio as the primary sources of information. For most of these students there was no special association with books or clear commitment to a liberal education—they came for careers and they wanted money and status to release them from their circumscribed backgrounds. Although their academic preparation was poorer than that of their predecessors and created sudden difficulties for the faculty, their urban profile was the same. They had scarcely left their neighborhoods to visit museums; they were

[2] The actual figures, taken from *The CUNY Data Book,* in 1976 and 1977, indicate the following ethnic pattern just before and during Open Admissions for all undergraduate students:

Year	White	Black	Hispanic	American Indian	Oriental	Other
1969	76.8	12.3	4.2	0.4	4.4	1.9
1970	64.7	20.5	6.6	0.2	5.2	2.8
1971	60.0	24.8	8.7	0.5	5.5	0.5
1972	55.8	22.0	11.8	0.4	5.6	4.4
1973	50.9	26.9	12.4	0.4	6.2	3.2
1974	38.8	31.5	15.0	0.4	6.7	7.6
1975	35.0	34.4	15.7	0.3	6.6	8.0
1976	32.8	34.8	21.1	1.0	10.3	—
1977	33.3	35.1	21.8	1.0	8.8	—

street smart but naïve about professions. Motivated. Aggressive. Determined to succeed. And now, in the early 1970s, burdened by poor preparation and aware of it—at times bitterly aware of it.

Imagine a young woman who wants to be a nurse. She has always had difficulty with writing; she sees little purpose in its relationship to her career, but she reluctantly takes the required Basic Writing 1 or 2; she resents her need, as an adult, to take this "elementary" subject which has plagued her all during her school years. Now she appears in a class where the instructor does not want to be, either, and where he wonders whether such a student does in fact need the skill of composition—at least in the short run. It is an unhappy alliance, one which does not bode well for a broad liberal arts education. . . .

Imagine a young man who is highly successful in understanding the concepts of his engineering classes but who cannot write well because he is foreign born; he dreams of rising to an executive position but knows that if he cannot write reports with a degree of clarity and accuracy, he will never go beyond a certain point in his career. His schedule is crowded, and the one or two courses in basic writing will not allow him to keep pace, linguistically, with the rigorous work demanded by the School of Engineering. . . .

Imagine a young woman who is driven to become an elementary school teacher and possesses all the human qualities appropriate for her profession but who, at the age of eighteen, still must struggle with basic writing. She knows she needs to be reasonably fluent if she is not to perpetuate her own linguistic problems in the students she teaches—but there is so little time in her program and the subject is painful and progress at this time in her life so difficult to measure. . . .

The problem of Open Admissions students that controlled all others was a weak command of the language. They needed a vast amount of attention in their attempt to master the writing of English. One could find some comprehension among them during the discussion of a reading assignment, and class sessions were animated with an intensity not experienced in the relevant sixties. The writing itself reflected that strong feeling, and on many occasions there were individual essays that promised sophistication beyond the grammatical difficulties; but, in general, the writing was so burdened with errors, it was difficult to find the time to work them out with the students, to see any coherent pattern behind the errors. The greatest task among many native-born blacks seemed to be that of verb tenses. Puerto Ricans and Asians had bilingual problems that often prevented them from reading conventional college texts and from writing college compositions; on occasion, a student would even arrive with an interpreter so that he could register for his classes. The white students, whose ethnicity was extremely varied, suffered from a general lack of basic skills. One wondered where all of them had been for the past twelve years.

Open Admissions students brought to their work a motivation that was like a hunger and that always seemed in conflict with poor academic preparation. I remember a

drug-dazed white girl in the sixties who slumped in her
seat, her guitar beside her, turned off by "irrelevant" education, while I tried to persuade her that *King Lear* was
worth reading. That scene was unimaginable in the seventies. Before Open Admissions, the range of performance in students was more graduated—one had a normal
distribution of grades, with a strong concentration of
"B's" and "C's." In the seventies, the distribution was
skewed more sharply—there were still some excellent students, but they now were coupled with large numbers of
the poorly prepared, and there were far fewer in the middle group.

At first, the underprepared were angry at their inadequacy; later, that anger subsided for most students and
the drill, the writing and rewriting, became the occu-
pation of the day. But there was always a passion for
learning among Open Admissions students, however elementary the learning might be, that never provoked the
use of a term like "relevance" or "purpose," so glibly uttered in the sixties. One was almost tempted to suggest
that the criterion for entrance to college be motivation,
not preparation or the ability to produce high scores. On
a human level, it was at times especially irritating to have
a seat occupied by a reasonably well-prepared but apa-
thetic student when it could have been filled by someone
hungry for the education—despite his lack of necessary
skills. But motivation is not measurable, and the experience of Open Admissions argues, most dramatically, that
adequate preparation is essential to success.

The need for students to master English was clear to

everyone; and on a fundamental level, instruction in basic writing was carried on intensively. In 1970, almost 90 per cent of City College students took some form of remedial instruction—an incredible situation for any American college. Seven hundred students were placed in Basic Writing 1 and seventeen hundred in Basic Writing 2. The other students enrolled in Basic Writing 3, the equivalent of our former freshman English.

Few people wanted to confront the unappealing implications of these language problems. They blamed the high school teachers, who blamed the junior high school teachers, who blamed the elementary school teachers, who blamed the parents, who blamed the schools, whose chairpersons and faculty and principals (many of them City College graduates) blamed us for having implemented Open Admissions and for not maintaining standards against which their students could measure themselves. When underemployed foreign language teachers were "retrained" for remedial work, most resisted it, and the students resisted them. When history teachers were used, they lectured on history to students who needed to know about subject and verb agreement. Faculty and administration were impatient with the work of teaching basic writing (it never seemed to produce "quantifiable" results) and acted as though it would eventually go away. But the subject proved to be the most difficult to teach— one that required a stretching of the imagination and tolerance rarely asked of "intellectuals." It also required that the teachers grow, too: a simple charge that they stop judging their students and attempt to understand them.

Many educators across the country were defending the student's "right to his own language," so that he would be protected against what was called "the cultural imperialism" of standard English. One read in the journals that black and Puerto Rican students would lose their idiosyncratic ethnicity, the special coloration of their language, their creativity. One listened to arguments against computerized America with its computerized language, the horrors of sociological jargon, the doublespeak of politicians, the Watergate grammar, the linguistic freakiness of Madison Avenue. A student's voice is his character, so the argument went, and should not be wholly lost in the supermarket language of bland and utilitarian America.

It was an interesting rhetorical argument, but a deceptive one—especially in regard to minority students whose proficiency at the standard language was tantamount to learning the art of breathing the special air of white America. The kind of deep creativity that is manifested in a private language—the blues or *Huckleberry Finn* or some of the poetry of Langston Hughes—is all the more powerful precisely because its vernacular is in a tension with standard public language. The two languages must be simultaneously held in the mind of the reader as well as of the writer, at whatever counterpoint can be productively sustained. Indeed, one reason why the language of creativity has lost its power is that the repressed emotions it once released are now on the public newsstands, debased by their high visibility. But one need not even explore any subtle notion about language and creativity—too much is at stake. For most students, writing is exposition, and exposition is standardized and should be clear (like Orwell's windowpane) and logical. It is the obligation of every English teacher to give students that primary skill.

At The City College we were too overwhelmed by the immensity of our problems to engage in theories about language acquisition. We never surrendered the conviction that our first obligation was to offer the conventional language conventionally, and we tried to teach these underprepared students in the same way as we had thousands of other freshmen. At the same time, we struggled to invent pedagogical devices that would make our teaching more effective. But despite all the good will that a lifetime of liberalism and academic training dictated, the nagging doubt grew that we might not be able to take an eighteen-year-old who suffered deep linguistic shortcomings and bring him to college-level verbal competence.

Many years have passed since this first attempt to merge a liberal arts education of the highest distinction with the demands of Open Admissions. Those of us who were asked to implement the enterprise strained so hard to be successful (as if the very essence of our liberal faith were being tested) that we didn't have the time to call into question the expectations imposed upon us by minorities and by ourselves. When our conservative colleagues screamed that the standards were falling, we answered by saying the record wasn't in yet. When we failed to bring students to the appropriate level of literacy, we blamed ourselves—we hadn't been adequately trained or we lacked patience or our standards were set too high too quickly.

But in fact we had false expectations. Those Open Admissions students who had severe problems in written expression came with a sense of fear and self-doubt, confronting a standard language that was rendered even more complicated by their need to master, at the same time and in the same place, the separate language of biology or psychology. Their entire miseducation and bookless past rose up to haunt them, and all the audio-visual aids and writing laboratories and simplified curriculum materials we tried could not work the miracle.

The mistake was to think that this language training would be preparation for college education when what we were really instilling was a fundamental literacy that would allow social acculturation to occur. We were preparing our students to be the parents of college students, not to be students themselves—trying to accomplish in one or two years' work that so involves the whole being it takes at least a generation to accomplish. Culture comes slowly; it cannot be force fed. And the impossible burden that we assumed was one properly meant for the community colleges of the City University.

The City College was in itself a university: a large College of Liberal Arts and Science, with divisions of humanities, social sciences, and sciences as well as Centers for Performing Arts and Legal Studies, Institutes for Medieval and Renaissance Studies and Oceanography, and a program in Women's Studies; a Center for Biomedical Education; professional schools of architecture, education, engineering, and nursing; a range of master's and doctoral programs, some based on campus, most co-ordinated with the City University Graduate Center at Forty-second Street; a School of General Studies; and, throughout the seventies, a large number of courses in basic skills. The enormous and necessary commitment to remediation strained the resources of the entire college.

Of course, the community colleges of the system— Manhattan, Queensboro, Kingsboro, Bronx, La Guardia, New York City, and Hostos—were overwhelmingly concerned with skills, too, and some students did transfer in their junior year, with adequate preparation and with ultimate success, into The City College or the other senior colleges of the system: Hunter, Brooklyn, Queens, John Jay, Staten Island, York, Lehman, Baruch, and Medgar Evers. But all of the senior colleges, to one extent or another, were compelled to establish programs in remediation, and the distinctions between community and senior colleges, in the first two years of work, were often blurred. The students who survived into their junior and senior years at City and the other senior colleges were no longer Open Admissions students—their competency in their chosen major as well as in basic skills was more than sufficient to prepare them for the professional demands of society.

Throughout the years, various educational leaders have recommended restructuring of the City University, and there have been commissions and committees and hearings on the subject; but the system has remained fundamentally the same. There is little point, therefore, in adding my own recommendations to the long list of others, but I should underscore my strong feeling that in the strictest sense, the two-year college—the most powerful phenomenon to appear in higher education during the past two decades—must be the direct bridge from the secondary school to the senior college. The community college is where the openness of Open Admissions should manifest itself, although I recognize that this level of education is in itself obviously too advanced for remedial instruction.

A far more comprehensive solution to our current problems in language acquisition is a sequential study of writing and literature, articulated between the different levels of education, from first grade through the second year of college—and this recommendation I discuss at some length in the last chapter. But until the earlier stages of education can bring students to the point where they have language skills adequate for a college education, public colleges in a democratic society have an obligation to educate as many students as they can accommodate. And this means that within an institution like the City University, the community colleges must be available to those who have the most severe problems, even if those two-year institutions replace some senior colleges; the four-year colleges cannot perform this task and still maintain programs and departments that offer what we consider to be a sophisticated education.

If a senior college does assume the massive burden of language instruction that The City College undertook in the 1970s, it either must alter most of its programs in the humanities and social sciences or face a student drift into "soft" subjects that do not require an exacting competence in language. At The City College, the traditional disciplines of philosophy and history and literature and political science diminished in significance and popularity because students felt unprepared for them. We expected too much too fast from our students. They had not been given a comfortable relationship to books at an early age so that learning had always seemed a struggle rather than a pleasure, something unnatural and unfamiliar. One should not be ashamed of educating the parents of college students—that is a worthy social function for any institution of learning—and if the society can simultaneously break down barriers of bias in employment and housing, a second generation will not experience, with so much intensity, this trauma that results from poor academic preparation.

One of the reasons why Open Admissions could never have succeeded completely was that it was imposed primarily and suddenly on education when education is only part of an intricate network of society—there must be open admissions everywhere for it to succeed in the classroom. And yet, despite the hasty implementation of Open Admissions and its consequent disorders, one must keep the record balanced: many students were brought to a level of achievement they (and their teachers) would never have thought possible; many were sensitized to the meaning of education, even though they may never have been graduated. This was not an ideal way to educate the children of the people, "the children of the whole people," and I will have many recommendations for improvement; but consider the alternative lives these underprepared students might have lived in an impossibly difficult job market.

Clouding the issues of literacy and Open Admissions, and every consequent question of how to provide a liberal arts education in an urban setting, was the sudden primacy of ethnicity and race. It conditioned everyone's response because it was central to the purpose of Open Admissions. In a college that had originally been almost entirely white and that by 1974 was more than half composed of minority students, race touched every educational issue—from black art to black journalism, from black history to black music. No record of this fitful period can be intelligible unless one understands the implications of racial tensions, vibrating at every meeting, working across and into the minds of everyone who cared.

IV

The dramatic moment came in the fall of 1971, at a large and raucous meeting of the Faculty Council, when new departments of ethnic studies were being considered. The room in which the meeting was held was one of the few at the college that had a seasoned, traditional beauty. It was on the second floor of Shepard Hall and was paneled with fine wood and framed by stained-glass windows and a high ceiling—an elegant, almost august room, where small concerts and lectures sometimes occurred. The chairs had a medieval character, heavy and lined with leather, and on a raised platform was a dais, with two very high chairs, rather like thrones, upon which the president and the Dean of Liberal Arts and Science sat.

That day, the two leaders of the college faced angry groups that had come with a clear purpose. The minorities wanted the power that departments represented, and they brought to the meeting dozens of students and friends and political figures from the Harlem community, who crowded the room, sitting on the floor and on window ledges.

The faculty that had to make the decision were white college professors whose parents were Irish and Italian and Jewish immigrants out of one ghetto or another, supporters of Roosevelt, Truman, and Stevenson. Most of them were still liberal and sympathetic to ethnic studies departments, as though they symbolized a retribution for past social sins. I myself had edited several books—*Dark Symphony: Negro Literature in America* and *A Nation of Nations*—and written many essays that insisted upon the significance of the ethnic perspective, the need to revise the curriculum so that it would go beyond only a representation of Western culture; and I had introduced courses into the English department before the ethnic revolution had even occurred. But I had the gravest reservations about the departmentalization of ethnicity. It was another step, it seemed to me, toward a politicized curriculum that could only harm the students it sought to serve. Some faculty were far more adamant, far more inflexible, and looked with open contempt on these newly created, non-traditional departments.

Several nights before the meeting of the Faculty Council, the president had held a briefing session in his home with all the chairpersons and critical administrators—ostensibly to seek their advice but really, as became clear, to prepare the vote. I had argued the case for integration and against the hasty implementation of new departments, but his mind was set, and he alluded to letters, external pressures, "a multi-ethnic institution" that reflected a multi-ethnic world, the shifting student population of the college. . . .

Like a thunder that speaks only to the emotions, the rhetoric rolled that October afternoon, and as the black and Puerto Rican and Asian spokesmen denounced our "racist" university in the midst of this "racist" society, the minority students (allowed to sit in the hall but not to participate) surrounded the white faculty members and cheered, clapped, and hissed until it became clear that reason would not prevail.

One white conservative rose to denounce the academic shallowness of ethnic departments and another mocked the arbitrary definition of a department (an ethnic group had to be represented by at least 5 per cent of the student body before applying for departmental status): Why only black, Puerto Rican, Asian, and Jewish departments? Why not Italian and Irish and Ukrainian? But the vocal white conservatives were small in number, even though their silent brothers and sisters were sizable. The conservatives were not the leaders of this campus. They had no students following them down the corridors and crowding their offices, and their loud protests fell on the embarrassed ears of squirming white liberals in the middle of the room.

Then the parade began. With black and Hispanic students seated round the room, like the inner ring of the enclosing black community, with non-tenured minority faculty confronting tenured white faculty, with the president of the college and the Dean of Liberal Arts and Science on the podium, the liberals rose vaguely and uncomfortably to express their sympathy for the creation of ethnic studies departments, regretting the haste with which they had been developed, of course, but still in sympathy. It was clear to me that black and white were the colors of the day, that the unknown (the interdisciplinary ethnic departments that cut across all bodies of knowledge to assert a racial or religious perspective) would ultimately have to coexist with the known (the clearly structured, power-based departments that represented the academic disciplines), and that gray was a color for the colorless. It was not the moment for subtlety or intellectual discrimination.

So, with the gravest misgivings about simple-minded ethnicity and politically oriented courses and mediocre faculty hired on the spot; with these private doubts aggravated by the thought that the creation of these departments *was* hasty, ill-conceived, an intellectual disgrace, and unfair to faculty and students—especially to future minority students for whom this college was being changed; but also with the unwillingness to be associated with academic reactionaries whose advocacy of "standards" and "excellence" seemed to be just another version of the superman syndrome (pronounced now by precisely those people who thirty years ago had been kept out of medical schools and Anglo-Saxon universities and all of the suburban country clubs)—with all of these contradictory emotions running through me, compounded by the personal disgust at the thought that I might be doing the bidding of an administration that simply wanted to solve a nasty problem as quickly as possible and by memories of having written about ethnic literature but of having been criticized by blacks for even touching these materials—I remembered Norman Mailer's easy remark that "Every compromise makes you less of a man," and I walked to the podium and compromised:

"We are being asked for an expression of faith in this administration that has dealt fairly with us on so many other matters. . . . I for one am ready to express that faith."

The departments were created, and the following months brought courses that could only encourage a militant separatism. New course descriptions were hurriedly presented before the curriculum committees for approval: "Organized and Disorganized Crime in the Black Community"; "The Contemporary Black Family" ("A normal Negro child, having grown within a normal family, will become abnormal on the slightest contact with the white world"); "The Prisoner as Political Hero"; "Protest and Rebellion Within Ante-Bellum America"; "Prisons and Concentration Camps" ("After Attica the entire system of corrections and penology must be re-examined"); "Seminars in Revolutionary Decolonization" ("The tradition of revolution as presented in classic portrayals of European and American experiences does not attempt to present the sociological basis of revolutions through a consistent theoretical analysis").

Each new course was a brick that heightened an academic wall between black studies and other programs of the college. With less intensity and self-conscious purpose and overt anger, many of the courses in the departments of Asian, Jewish, and Puerto Rican studies served to further the same insular tendency. Each of these groups developed some courses that were valuable in themselves, but they also developed, despite their efforts, an effect of self-isolation, a defensiveness that too often took the form of petty academic politics.

Now a decade has passed and the fire has not burned us, after all—although some extraordinary leaders have been killed. But it has singed our sensibilities in ways not easily forgotten. The academic home we live in has been altered to accommodate other voices in other rooms and, with luck, in our own rooms. That passionate intensity experienced on so many college campuses was an attempt to establish racial bases of power within an educational structure that was controlled by a white, male, fundamentally European perspective. Now that the fire has subsided, it is possible to draw a few conclusions that may seem rational.

The creation of ethnic studies departments at The City College and throughout the nation developed, like Open Admissions itself, from the fact that educators had not confronted, in any meaningful way, the reality of American society. They had not invited the participation of ethnic groups or pointed a way toward the integration of ethnicity into the curriculum or responded imaginatively to the racial revolution that had been occurring in this nation since at least 1954. Then, when forced to deal with the sudden insistence on ethnic representation, too many educators capitulated to the extreme political pressure of some minority leaders or sabotaged the genuine efforts of others. Once black studies was established, Puerto Rican, Asian, and Jewish studies had to follow; and before long, courses in ethnic history and sociology and literature were conflicting with those of the traditional departments. The result, with few exceptions, is a curriculum that has the faculty of ethnic studies ghettoized in separate corners of the colleges, even though most students major in the more traditional disciplines and some faculty members do have joint appointments with departments of sociology and political science. Each ethnic group is sorely tempted to raise its own consciousness at the expense of general education. Attempts to develop courses and programs in comparative ethnicity have failed, and the minorities in these departments feel more alienated than before.

Creating ongoing departments in the formal structure of the college was wrong, and those with empty hands are the minorities for whom they were created. Conservatives from the traditional departments were not displeased at the isolation of the new departments, for they suspected that Open Admissions pupils—the less well-prepared pupils—would segregate themselves in ethnic studies departments while the intellectually secure and confident students would remain in their own discipline-oriented departments. The well-intentioned liberals agreed to the creation of these departments out of no deep ideological impulse, with no real purpose or passion. They accepted the change cynically, and mocked its results privately. They accepted it because to do so was easy. And like the society, the college became fragmented and divided.

The representation of ethnicity was understandable in the sixties and early seventies, coming after years of denial and indifference by the majority culture. Like most movements of this sort in American history, it was far too extreme, but it did offer a unique perspective, long undervalued in our education. It asserted to all of us who had been trained in Western European culture that the future of world civilization will depend upon an understanding of China and India and Japan and the countries of Africa and South America. Anyone who has traveled in these distant places—though not so distant any longer in our global village—must be impressed by how much the people know about Americans and how little we know about them. It is a cultural arrogance we can scarcely afford.

Within the American continent itself, a sensitivity to ethnicity was and is a humanizing force—one of many safeguards against our final homogenization and loss of uniqueness—but it cannot become an end in itself, for then it becomes divisive; it cannot glorify race or religion, for then it becomes antidemocratic and self-isolating. Educationally, ethnicity should have proceeded in the form of courses that ultimately penetrate the curriculum and alter its perspective; a transitional movement that insists upon integration while it maintains its discrete characteristics. The ethnic point of view must finally be an angle of our comprehensive vision that does not claim to be something separate, a *personal* matter that does not lose its hard-won uniqueness by becoming merely a group effort or struggle. Surely this is one lesson learned from the history of racism in America: to form a separate colony or country or state or, in the academy, a separate department is to weaken the effort, to fight the social vortex of this democracy, to sacrifice the dignity that can only come through a total integration into and reshaping of the curriculum. Orlando Patterson, a Harvard sociologist, has put the case well:

> Ethnic pluralism, however dressed up in liberal rhetoric, has no place whatever in a democratic society based on the humanistic ideals of our Judaeo-Christian ethic. It is, first, socially divisive. However much the more liberal advocates of the revival may proclaim the contrary, the fact remains that the glorification of one's heritage and one's group always implies its superiority, its "chosenness" over all others.
>
> Second, the ethnic revival is a dangerous form of obfuscation. There are indeed many severe problems in our society but interpreting them in psycho-cultural terms immediately obscures the real issues such as poverty and unemployment in the midst of affluence, racism, sexism and environmental assault. These are tough issues requiring tough-minded and rational solutions as well as unswerving commitment to equality and human fraternity. We do not solve

them by idle talk about the "twilight of authority" or by searching for largely fanciful roots.

Ethnicity emphasizes the trivialities that distinguish us and obscures the overwhelming reality of our common genetic and human heritages as well as our common needs and hopes. By emphasizing differences, ethnicity lends itself to the conservative belief in the inevitability of inequality. It is no accident that the neo-conservative thinkers have all hailed the revival.

. . . Profoundly anti-American in its anti-individualism, the ethnic revival celebrates diversity, not however of individuals but of the groups to which they belong. It is a sociological truism that the more cohesive an ethnic group, the more conformist or the more anti-individualistic are its members. Thus the call for a diversity of cohesive, tightly knit groups actually amounts to an assault on the deeply entrenched principle of individualism.

. . . The time has come when all genuine humanists who cherish the great ideal of the Constitution—that all human beings are created equal—must awake from their slumber and meet head on the challenge of the chauvinists.

At Columbia University in the 1950s, during the time I studied for a Ph.D. in American literature, no black author was on any list of readings—and this phenomenon was true of most graduate schools in the country. It seemed extraordinary, but in those years one questioned nothing in the curriculum, certainly not the awesome faculty of scholars who created that curriculum or the administration of Columbia University that granted the degree. One studied the required readings for the required examinations in order to leave the place as soon as possible.

It took the average person twelve years to receive the Ph.D. from Columbia. Most students were eliminated at the master's level and the survivors went through a series of examinations: three foreign languages; the history of the English language; Anglo-Saxon, Chaucer, oral examinations before boards of six examiners; a dissertation to be approved by three faculty readers and then defended before six other examiners. This educational obstacle course had little apparent relationship with classroom teaching at The City College, but by the time one received one's doctorate from Columbia one knew English and American literature in a way that provided the fundamental confidence of a lifetime—to one's students and oneself. One knew the quality of superb writing and thought, against which other writing and thought could be measured. One had the dignity of a profession—books to be written, classes to be taught, college service to be rendered. One had succeeded in a most elite academic structure and despite one's egalitarian protest, one was proud to have succeeded. The gift of Columbia was an unshakable intellectual authority carried through a life in which too few people achieve anything of which they are proud; the gift was a respect for the intellect, for the play of mind, for ideas. It was not the ideal instant preparation for Open Admissions and it was narrowly conservative and snobbish, but it had a standard of excellence no one ever found confusing.

The Open Admissions students themselves knew there

was the power of a broad and deep education behind one's correction of a simple composition. They knew their instructor was also teaching a course in Shakespeare or modern American literature and they wanted him to have the power of that education, and to preserve the excellence that Columbia represented. Still, the highly elaborate, self-contained form of education at Columbia—at least in American literature—was not sufficiently responsive to black culture or democratic culture generally and, as a consequence, made itself vulnerable to the criticisms of the sixties. It was far too aloof from the immediate society into which its young scholars and future classroom teachers would soon be professionally engaged.

As a student of American literature at Columbia, I should not have had to discover Frederick Douglass, W. E. B. Du Bois, Langston Hughes, Richard Wright, Ralph Ellison, and James Baldwin by myself—not when I was required to read second-rate white writers, many of them local colorists who, like Thomas Nelson Page and Joel Chandler Harris, commented benignly upon black America. My closest black friend at Columbia was discouraged from writing his dissertation on Langston Hughes. He wrote the essay anyway because he happened to be older than most graduate students and tough and persistent and absolutely clear in his values; an expanded version of that dissertation was ultimately published as a book. It is appalling that the two of us, black and white, sharing a seminar on American culture in Philosophy Hall at Columbia University in the late 1950s, never discussed the literature of American Negroes—the literature of that race which Richard Wright once called America's metaphor. We had to grope our way toward the publication of a book, ten years later, that recognized the literary quality of black American authors.

Our book appeared in the late sixties, when black studies departments developed on campuses across the country. Now, ten years later, after the riots and burnt-out buildings and student take-overs, the curriculum at Columbia (and even more extensively at city and state colleges) has integrated blackness, so that the movement of ethnic studies, in its original form, has served its purpose. Columbia University suffered from a deleterious and inexcusable conservatism before 1960. It did not provide a scholarship for American society; it did not anticipate the need of minorities, or recognize their rights; it excluded minority literature from the curriculum; it waited for the society to compel its direction. No wonder so many of us felt hollow in our hearts after having admired and emulated, with our heads, the literary elegance of "the liberal imagination." Still, the reaction against doctoral work —at Columbia and elsewhere—became, in the 1960s, so great a reaction against the mind itself that many humanists no longer believed in their disciplines and ran after relevance, and broke up the curriculum entirely, obscuring those exacting standards that Columbia had always represented.

American education—American culture at large—is finally integrative, and the subject matter cannot be obfuscated in the name of ethnic heritage or women's studies or homosexual studies or experimental studies—not if these "studies" are primarily political and insist upon a programmatic definition. The appropriation of knowledge for some personal need is one reality. That is the reason most of us have for learning anything, and the passion black students bring to the study of American culture is not rivaled by their white counterparts, for it is aggressively critical. But to use knowledge solely to further a cause will ultimately debase the knowledge because it is being manipulated for a narrow purpose. The student is allowed to evade personal responsibility and unique humanity for an abstraction that has an absolute quality and a finality; the student's use of his knowledge is too predictable, too tendentious; it contradicts self-reliance.

It is insufficient to say—as defenders of these programs do say—that a college teaches students, not subject matter, and that therefore students should explore what they wish, however they wish. This is a sentimental, passive argument, so relativistic and shifting that it blurs an essential educational vision, that judges priorities, that sets forth objectives and skills, that knows its own inherent meaning. It offers the students themselves—no more, no less. It offers no leadership. It points in no direction.

V

The full implications of Open Admissions had little meaning for people at either end of the educational spectrum: those who advocated a narrow ethnicity and those who for so long had considered themselves the custodians of an unvarying culture. Even those who supported professional education most vigorously failed to acknowledge the need for vast resources to improve the language skills of the new undergraduates. Scientists claimed that too many students were placed in basic writing courses and accused the English department of self-aggrandizement, of shoring up its British Empire; social scientists continued to give short-answer tests. The liberal arts faculty complained about expensive professional programs for bright students, whom they never saw in their classrooms, and about students in remedial classes, whom they did not want to teach.

Where were the old liberal arts students who simply wanted to study philosophy and literature and history? Where were those who could not be programmed, who weren't so absolutely certain of their careers, who weren't so utterly nervous about job security, and who came to us with a literacy we took for granted? Gone. Gone to colleges of the state university. Gone to private colleges. Gone to the suburbs and the exurbs and the hinterlands, where (we soon would learn) colleges confronted similar problems: the vast majority of educated and middle-class students were also enrolled in professional and business programs—more than 70 per cent of the students across the country—rather than the liberal arts. And with their flight something had faded from our own lives—a passing purpose, a pointed passion. More. What really gnawed away at our innards and left us hollow, what began to create a sad yet anxious look in our eyes and a dreadful listlessness in the way we moved through classes or sat at committee meetings, protected by institutional reports, what dulled our lunchroom conversation and made us depend more on each other than on the students—who had always been the great reward for teaching at The City College—what coursed in our bodies like an incurable illness was our growing realization and fear that in middle age we no longer had a profession.

Elective courses in literature, languages, philosophy, and history attracted only a handful of students, and though we defended the study of the humanities in the most elegant rhetoric, fewer and fewer students were interested in our subjects. Those few who might have cared had no incentive to prepare for graduate school since teaching jobs were unavailable. The number of "majors" plummeted so that the professional perpetuation and legacy of our disciplines could not be transmitted to a younger generation of acolytes. Worse still, most students were no longer motivated to read—assignments grew shorter and even those were rarely read. In desperate measures redolent of Madison Avenue, the faculty created sexy courses to attract students: Gay literature; Jewish fertility. Then they tried to sell the courses with gaudy posters or notices in campus newspapers. In the sweaty gym, during registration, too many faculty were no better than barkers at a circus sideshow touting the attractions awaiting behind the tent flap. Once the student buyers were in the classes, the pressure to inflate grades, to be permissive with those who cut classes, to make allowances for late papers was irresistible. The national competition for students was eroding the quality of American higher education generally, public as well as private, as colleges attempted to seduce students away from one another. The same competitive effect was now taking place within the nineteen branches of CUNY and within the thirty-five departments of The City College. Student enrollment determined departmental strength. College had become a kind of cheap academic stock market, and teachers were stockbrokers in an inflationary educational economy.

All of these forces developed, Pelion upon Ossa, a scramble for infinite options to satisfy every taste or lack of taste, until the college bulletin resembled the smashed windows of a very large house that once had been considered home. An academic home. There was no vision, however singular it might have been, that offered a future to the educators and that would return the faculty members' professions to them. The numbers that constituted a class were appalling: professional education for 700 students who majored in architecture, education, engineering, nursing, biomedicine, law, and performing arts; 1,700 who needed remedial work; and a handful of students in liberal arts and sciences who were genuinely ready for a college education—now they were called honors students.

The natural tendency was to expand the professional programs and view liberal education deductively: to establish a career goal and then shape the education accordingly. The general economic condition of the city and country encouraged parents, students, and educators to move in this direction—to clutch at what seemed to be survival in a confusing age. The study of language, literature, philosophy, history, physics, and mathematics on their own terms seemed impossible, given the desires and needs of students, given the pressures of a decaying city, given the budget (which finally ran out, forcing the City University to close on May 28, 1976, for two weeks while we listened to wrangling politicians and lined up, for the first time in our lives, for unemployment compensation). As each career program was established, the traditional disciplines in liberal arts and sciences were placed in a service relationship to vocationalism—as though the only way they could be made interesting or relevant was by attaching them to practical programs. The fundamental center of a liberal education, as we had always known it, was in danger, and it was clear that the college might soon become something other than an institution of higher learning: a training ground for young specialists who would acquire no sense of the wholeness that binds together the learning experience that must be a preparation for life, not just for earning a living.

For the way of earning a living, I knew, might easily change. The job market would change. It was changing so rapidly that training someone for one job was not preparing him for something else that would appear moments after he was graduated. With each new crisis I became more convinced that a college had to be greater than the sum of its parts—more than simply a series of vocational programs; and it could not be so if there were not a deep, self-consciously stated commitment to liberal arts and sciences, if there were not a statement to all of our community—but particularly to our students—that we believed it essential to study in certain central fields of knowledge. Without this conviction that a university is a place of ideas rather than an institution concerned primarily with the preparation for careers, the educational center would not hold and professional programs would have no intellectual touchstone for their own reality. Without this conviction there would be no authority of intellect, no educational vision; pragmatism would reign; vocational programs would shift like products in the marketplace; and the shadows on the wall of the cave would become more real than the fire.

Inevitably one returns in education to the basic questions of what the student *knows* upon graduation and especially what skills of interpretation he possesses. If he does not know something of philosophy and history; if he has not developed critical skills that distinguish the moral from the immoral, flatulent language from genuine, art from artifact—then he is not educated. Discrimination is essential; intellectual discrimination. That and lengthening the critical attention span, so atomized by television and radio and newspapers and a hundred forces colliding with the eye and the ear. And acquiring the understanding of a few great texts—a few will suffice—that have lived beyond their moment in time. And achieving the self-reliance that grows from the authority of knowing some things well.

There is a distancing essential in a college education. Many educators consumed with relevance and impatient with the hesitancies of the university, have scoffed at the ivory towers, the colleges set off on grassy knolls away from the busy world; but this distancing, for four years in a person's life, is not altogether absurd—an intellectual distancing, if a physical one is impossible. This is not to say that action is extrinsic to the educational process—on the contrary; but it must develop organically from thought, in the terms of an educator like Horace Mann, and not be a substitute for thought. A college should teach a student to think straight and see perceptively. But one cannot see if he is constantly watching the contemporaneous world, nose against the windowpane, so immersed in its dailiness and its sociology that he loses what was once called perspective. Knowledge is certainly not enough. It should lead to wisdom, which carries vision in its meaning, and in many of its manifestations it should result in social action. But without knowledge, wisdom is hard bought and social action founded on uninformed judgments. Knowledge cannot be only the sociology and economics and political science of the moment, ever shifting, stimulating an anxiety that stems from uncertainty, fogged by statistics that carry with them apparent truth. Without a past, what future can we have? And the purpose of the humanities is to offer the student a past which illuminates the present moment upon which he can build a future.

Now, in the seventies, the dangers of vocationalism are as real as the mindless pursuit of relevance and the political pressures to replace education with ethnic chauvinism. As the problems of Open Admissions prove to be intractable and a conventional liberal arts education appears less than purposeful to students because of limited job opportunities, the new vocationalism has become superficially attractive—to humanists who are naturally distressed that they are losing customers to professional schools and to career-oriented administrators who see professionalized education as an instant solution to these knotty problems. At The City College, paralyzed by what seemed a never-ending budget crisis, the impulse toward career education was particularly intense, and most intense for those of us who wished to preserve the humanities in some form that resembled their original purpose.

VI

My role as Dean of Humanities was to support the development of a master plan which the president had envisaged for The City College: an urban educational model that would make the connection between the professions students wanted and the liberal education they needed. The president was a physicist, who had come out of poverty in the Bronx, traveled briefly through the old City College, then Columbia and Cornell, and spent the better part of his career at the University of Rochester solving sophisticated problems in high energy physics and, as chairman, developing a physics department of great distinction. Now he had returned to New York, a college president with a liberal disposition whose primary problem was to prevent The City College from yielding so completely to the enormous demands of remediation in English and mathematics that there would be no resources left for the rest of the institution and for the implementation of his urban educational model.

For eight years, in an attempt to counteract the force of Open Admissions and to build a future for the college that would connect with the needs of New York City, the president established professional programs that were intrinsically excellent but that, together with the growing and forced commitment to remediation, strained to survive. And at the center of this struggle between egalitarianism and elitism was the large traditional College of Liberal Arts and Science—the great legacy of The City College that the alumni and the faculty remembered. A bitter conflict ensued between the president's every attempt to develop his new programs and the faculty's efforts to preserve the legacy they had known as well as to protect their personal future through the disciplines they had always taught. In addition to the existing schools of education, engineering, nursing, and architecture, programs in biomedicine, legal studies, and performing arts were implemented. With the development of each new program the faculty balked, for fear that this direction toward career education might make them the victims of what could quickly become a vocational school, of what was promptly demeaned as "social engineering."

But the president was not interested in a narrow vocationalism. His intention was more far-reaching than simply the retention of those bright students who had always been the pride of City College. The real goal was the development of what he called "an urban educational model" that would help build a multi-ethnic middle class. The fate of City College had always been linked inextricably to the fate of New York itself, and were there time enough and money, the president felt that students could be trained in accelerated programs as doctors and lawyers and nurses and architects so as to improve the quality of life in a city that had lost so many middle-class families to the suburbs. The perplexing, nagging question was whether an urban college could respond so directly to the social diseases of its environment, especially when burdened by the educational and fiscal demands of Open Admissions. But the very question seemed self-indulgent —a humanist's abstraction of a human problem, a retreat from social reality as disconcerting as that of the Columbia liberals in the fifties and sixties. New York City was disintegrating so rapidly that academic questions seemed beside the point. Imagination and intelligence had to serve social purpose or what was the meaning of humanism? One could no longer afford to be an academic humanist in anything like the conventional sense, and the only role that seemed appropriate was that of activist.

From the moment the president drafted his urban educational model, I became one of its greatest champions; for whatever the internal difficulties presented to a beleaguered college faculty, I knew that his was the proper educational response to urban problems, however incomplete it might ultimately prove to be. I knew that he had given up the comfortable life of a research physicist—a distinguished professor in a wealthy, private university— to turn his intelligence and energy toward the social problems of the urban poor. No academic battlefield could have been more charged with the crossfire of conflicts in class and race and sex and educational philosophy—the turbulence of the times—than The City College of the City University of New York in the 1970s. For no college had changed so dramatically so quickly. And I, as a humanist and full professor chose to turn the intelligence that I possessed toward the solution of these problems. It seemed a humanistic contradiction to be teaching at The City College and not be engaged in something like an urban educational model. . . . So the scientist and the humanist met in that unlikely spot, with its tired old buildings from the turn of the century and its temporary facilities from the late 1960s—we met in that unlikely academic city upon a hill.

The forces that resisted the implementation of the urban educational model were, at times, overwhelming. One expected a recalcitrant faculty, for in the seventies, because of economic problems that constantly threatened tenure, faculties were more conservative than administrators. Of greater concern was the unwillingness of middle-class parents to send their children to Harlem, despite the appeal of the programs. The subway ride through the labyrinthine tunnels of New York was a journey into danger—no public relations from the college could counteract this public anxiety. Whereas The City College had always attracted the "brightest and the best" students in New York, they now went to the various branches of the State University of New York. The City College was identified as the senior college of Open Admissions, and only by connecting the programs in biomedicine and law with later professional training in actual hospitals and law schools—and ultimately to high-paying careers—could we hope to attract two or three hundred students of traditionally high caliber.

These programs had several features that were appealing: they were accelerated so that students could complete their undergraduate education and professional training within six rather than the usual eight years; they attempted to integrate liberal arts courses with those of the vocational disciplines; most importantly, they insisted that the students serve the urban community, the urban poor, after they completed their course of study. This last feature was a strong consideration in the interview process; indeed, the entering biomedical student was required to sign a contract that he would spend a prescribed period of time practicing medicine in the city after graduation from the program. Of course, there was no absolute guarantee that this social mission would be honored, but it was so organically fused into the curricula and summer internships that one could be more than moderately optimistic.

The other great difficulty in the development of an urban educational model was the inherent expense of professional programs—especially the biomedical. Tax-levy funds had been radically reduced by a city that seemed (in 1973) to be moving inexorably toward fiscal collapse—one never knew the extent of the budget until a month before the academic year began and then it was slashed in mid-year by upstate legislators. In order to implement the urban educational model and to assure an anxious faculty that no tax-levy dollars would be used for any of these programs, the president launched a $25-million fund-raising campaign. Modest by normal standards—but the first real drive of this sort by a college that now would become, if successful, private as well as public.

The approaches to alumni, foundations, and federal agencies began in a desperate race against time, for in effect we had lost faith in the city to recover itself through its own revenues. Trapped in a period of deceleration, we had developed the habit of discussing the budget only in terms of who should be fired, what operating cost reduced, where we could effect savings—and I always seemed to be studying data that indicated the enrollment in humanities was suffering. Negative thinking in a city that seemed incapable of self-government, self-improvement, and self-respect. The phoenix would not rise from the ashes of Times Square, the South Bronx, the Village, the Bowery, or Harlem: we had to discover it in the alumni of the college, in the friends of this experiment called Open Admissions. We turned outward for financial support to strengthen ourselves internally, and we seemed to have a chance at success that very few colleges—and almost no other public urban college—could dare to imagine.

Here was a City College with a 125-year-old tradition that elicited great pride from an alumni body as influential as that of almost any college in America. This was not Harvard—The City College had no real experience in sophisticated fund-raising and it had no social panache—but it had indeed been a proletarian Harvard that could still make you gasp when you regarded the lists of its graduates: A. M. Rosenthal, the executive editor of the New

York *Times;* Jonas Salk, inventor of the polio vaccine; Simon Rifkind and Stanley Fuld, lawyers and judges; Herman Badillo, congressman and then deputy mayor; Seymour Lipset, Nathan Glazer, Daniel Bell, Irving Kristol, the social scientists; A. Philip Randolph; Arthur Kornberg, the biochemist, Kenneth Arrow, the economist, Robert Hofstadter, the physicist, and Julius Axelrod, the biologist—all Nobel Prize winners; Leonard Davis, Chairman of the Board of the Colonial Penn Insurance Group; Arnold Picker, former chairman of the board at United Artists; Bernard Malamud and Paddy Chayevsky and Yip Harburg and Ira Gershwin and Alfred Kazin and Irving Howe and Edward Kosner. And on and on and on—so many New Yorkers, from 1920 to 1970, had some association with The City College—to form a roster of more than 100,000 living alumni as distinguished as that of any in an American college. But in addition to having achieved great distinction in American life, most of these alumni had an intense sensitivity to urban problems. They wanted to help solve the difficulties the president identified; they were smart enough to realize that Open Admissions was an inevitable responsibility of The City College, although many of them were troubled by the radical decline in the academic quality of students; and, most valuably, they wanted to repay a debt to the college.

Some alumni, whose life styles had grown affluent, needed to forget that they had ever passed through The City College—it reminded them of a poverty they did not find romantic, and if they had gone to a graduate or business or professional school like Columbia or the University of Pennsylvania, their loyalties were to the private institution. But the overwhelming majority of graduates felt a debt that was personal and profound. When I served as Vice-president for Institutional Advancement and spoke to many of these leaders, I heard a theme that could have been the history of twentieth-century New York. "If it had not been for the presence of City College I would never have gone to college. As simple as that. Columbia and N.Y.U. were financially out of the question. City College was the only possibility—it existed alone for me—and if not for that college, I would not be here in this office, talking to you. As simple as that. Now, what can I do for you?" And after I had suggested what they could do for me—for The City College—they suddenly grew much older and more pragmatic. "I will pay back my debt—but I can only go so far. Remember, I have many, many other obligations."

The great problem, for the fund-raiser, was a fairly typical one: harnessing the good will of these alumni and persuading them to raise The City College obligation higher on their list of obligations. But the problem was aggravated by several overwhelming facts that alumnus after alumnus presented: "Why should I give large sums of private money to a public institution? More importantly, how can I give money to a public institution that never knows, from year to year, what its budget will be, although it is almost certain that the budget will diminish? Not your fault, mind you, but there is no base of support for a sensible investment. . . . I'll increase my annual giving, but . . ."

Despite the difficulty of answering these questions honestly, of creating an image of possibility in the face of what seemed insuperable odds (first the state threatened to withdraw support, then the city), the president launched his $25-million campaign with great energy and belief. Even before the official campaign began, there had been hopeful signs. In 1971, the wealthiest living alumnus had called the president to volunteer a gift of $2.6 million to establish a Center for Performing Arts; a few years later he provided the seed money for a highly competitive biomedical program. . . . For more than seven years, I sat at meetings with the president and the donor, who had acquired his enormous fortune within one generation. A decent man who remembered his roots. I watched the donor regard the incredible fiscal problems of The City College of New York and still retain his fundamental belief in its future for the poor children who were now primarily black and Hispanic and Asian. . . .

These programs and their full or partial funding were in various stages of development when the official capital gifts campaign began. As Dean of Humanities, I watched the genesis of the fund-raising drive: mountains of materials being shaped to build a "case," bright brochures produced, grants and proposals developed, consultants brought in to advise the president and his staff. Suddenly, I was in the middle of it, at least for a year—the president had asked me to head up the campaign.

The request came shortly after thirty-three faculty had been fired in the Humanities Division, weeks after the university had been closed because of insufficient funds, in the dog days of summer 1976, when I realized, with cold clarity, that it would be years before this college could recover from a fiscal bloodbath that had left the college almost fully tenured and with fewer and fewer students. I had gone on a trip for a summer month, to recover from a depressing year during which a blue-ribbon faculty committee had consulted with every administrator about the best way to sacrifice fifty-nine careers and had drawn up a cogent document of options and then, when the firings came, had watched us proceed (as everyone knew we would) in terms of seniority among the non-tenured staff. Twelve in English . . . seven in Romance Languages . . . eight or nine in Speech . . . like deaths reported from a battlefront. And these young men and women, who had Ph.D.'s and publications and deserved an academic future, caucused with their union representatives to build a case against the university when they knew they had no case—no legal case—not even a moral case: the budget was too low to afford them, there weren't enough students for them to teach. Already they were scrambling for other jobs, everywhere, anywhere. . . .

As I entered my hotel, the president's packages greeted me—thick documents describing the background to the campaign, the achievements, the goals, the lists of alumni at different levels of potential giving. . . .

In September I was in the thick of it. . . .

One of the most important attorneys in America has agreed to host a meeting in his Park Avenue offices for thirty corporate executives, the most distinguished and powerful City College graduates. Four show up to hear the case for the urban educational model. The others are too busy or out of town or not interested. . . . We try a President's Club, but that too is not successful. . . . Then we hit upon the program that is most attractive to alumni: City College Scholarships, intended to bring better-prepared high school students to the college. The president and I have dozens of meetings with wealthy graduates who are in a position to endow a $25,000 scholarship or have their companies endow it—breakfast and luncheon meetings on Wall Street and in midtown and at the president's home, advocating the future of City College as the newspapers report the financial uncertainty of the university, promoting this program, that institute, changing the topic as a potential donor's interest changes and talking suddenly of endowed chairs or perhaps a lecture series or a special program or naming a building, a room, a library collection. We draw upon every human and institutional resource to convince alumni that The City College has a future. . . .

The president and I try to persuade a group of distinguished humanists to establish the new National Humanities Center in New York—"not in some sylvan retreat but here in New York, for if the humanities survive, they will have to survive in the city"—and we quote Eric Hoffer and they listen with consideration and take the center to a sylvan retreat in North Carolina. "Mr. President, the humanist needs to have the peace of mind to write a book on Plato, too." . . . Proposals for minorities in engineering, for legal studies and biomedicine and communications and health technology—trying to develop a financial base of millions, although millions will never be enough, not when The City College tax-levy budget is $47 million one year, then within two years $35 million, and the college is fully tenured and the enrollment continues to decline. . . .

The three-year campaign is extended to five years; the scholarship program is quite successful; there is an endowed chair, partially funded, in legal studies. The campaign stops and goes, but even so, the successes are extraordinary given the discouraging fiscal context in which the campaign has been conducted. And the idea of having a public/private university, of asking the corporate sector to aid a publicly financed institution in building a future for the city in which they both live—this idea, and all the others it has spawned, is certainly one fundamental way to resolve our urban crises. It will not cure the language problems Open Admissions students now bring to senior colleges, but it will provide funds to allow college instructors the time and resources necessary for work in training teachers and college tutors, in establishing summer programs that improve the language skills of all students, and in developing curricula—recommendations outlined in the final chapter. Beyond Open Admissions, the public/private university can provide the professionals so desperately needed in medicine, law, and public service—training that should be a shared responsibility of the public and private sectors of the economy.

The urban educational model and its fund-raising campaign were extraordinary efforts to transcend the fiscal difficulties that beset The City College. In another time, with a more stable budget, and with a student body better prepared to act upon its possibilities, it might have succeeded. But the never-ending, agonizing problem for this senior college, carrying on a range of subjects that demanded real competence in language and arithmetic—the problem that clouded every effort—was rooted in Open Admissions. And by treating the problem of literacy in English and mathematics as a burden rather than a central mission, the urban educational model of the seventies missed its greatest, most profound opportunity. The demand for the improvement of language skills was a task suddenly imposed upon all of us, out of political exigencies—no one really had an educational choice—and one could not make obvious and necessary distinctions between the sort of education compatible with the mission of a senior college, as opposed to that of a junior college or even of pre-college institutes concentrating upon remediation; but once the task was ours, we should have brought to it greater imagination and energy and belief than we did.

VII

The seventies will be remembered, at The City College and at all the city colleges of America, as the era of Open Admissions. That was its special signature. For a decade Americans became especially aware of the language difficulties the new generation suffered from. They were told of declining scores on the national S.A.T. examinations; of the pejorative impact of television; of a technological age that devalued books; of students who had great difficulties in the simple expression of ideas; and they read the plethora of articles that lamented Johnny's inability to read and write. But the most dramatic reason that literacy became a national problem was the opening of admissions everywhere, the democratization of higher education.

The most serious question confronting American education pressed upon The City College and the City University with a devastating rapidity. What would be the essence of a college education in a time of economic retrenchment, in an institution that would have to be committed to a continued form of Open Admissions, in the latter part of twentieth-century America?

The answer to that question is simple if one denies the need for Open Admissions and proceeds from a position of exclusivity that disregards the greater demand for higher education within the past ten years, particularly by minorities. The argument is familiar and has an inexorable logic. Exclude the unprepared through tests that insist upon the highest standards and send them into jobs that do not require literacy. Those who haven't performed well by the time they apply to college don't belong there anyway. That is the way it has always been; that is the way it is in most countries of the world; that is the way it should be, especially in a time of economic difficulties. Higher education is a privilege, not a right.

For a long time, of course, this was the policy, *de facto*, at The City College of New York. But it is one thing to speak of free tuition and democratic education in a City University of four senior colleges that impose the most vigorous criteria for admissions. That educational framework is probably as close an approximation as Americans have yet made to Jefferson's "natural aristocracy," his "aristocracy of talent"—and it functions on the premise of exclusive admissions. It is another matter to speak of ten senior colleges, seven community colleges, a graduate center, a total population at one time of 270,000 students, reduced now to 175,000; that is an extraordinary commitment to democratic education. Truly Open Admissions. At some point, clearly, quantity affects quality. If one believes in opening the doors of higher education to everyone who wants to enter—and in a democracy, is there ultimately any choice?—any true answer to the question of what a liberal education ought to be, that goes beyond rhetoric and the usual pieties, must first come to terms with the illiteracy that is ravaging American society.

Twenty per cent of the adults in our country are functionally illiterate—and an additional twenty per cent, at least, cannot read simple directions on food boxes. There is, as one observer has remarked, a "glacial drift away from the printed word," and if it continues "we could conceivably wind up with a society in which reading and writing were specialist arts, the skills of an intellectual minority." The spiritual, cultural, and political dangers of illiteracy to our democracy are clear; but consider the danger to us all if newspapers and magazines, so important in disseminating specific information, were reduced in circulation and in number; consider a government forced to "protect" its people by regulating consumer products because vast numbers cannot read labels or directions. A future for the humanities in American education and society must begin with literacy.

Beyond literacy, even high literacy, and the acquisition of interpretative skills that result from careful reading, the essence of a college education in America depends upon our willingness to say that certain disciplines are primary, others secondary—that (for example) philosophy, history, literature, economics, physics, and mathematics are central. It depends upon our belief in the university as a place of the mind and not a social agency or a supermarket selling whatever is popular. A university has an obligation to place before its students the great ideas of human history, written in their most memorable prose and poetry. When it ceases to do that, it ceases to be a university. This must be true not only of private institutions that have a homogeneous student body, but of large, sprawling urban universities where educational coherence is far more difficult to achieve and sustain. Having asserted the centrality of the liberal arts in any curriculum, one must make the very difficult connection with professional education and the careers students want defined for them at earlier and earlier stages of their development. I attempt an organic connection with pre-professional education—an outline of a synthesis for the humanities—in the final chapter of this book.

At the same time, and on the same asphalt campus in Chicago or Los Angeles or New York or in towns across this country, the university in a democracy must be an

open place, like a church or a library, where people linger
for a moment in their lives, and enlighten their lives, and
enlighten the lives of others who may follow them. For it
is clear that the development of skills and the acquisition
of knowledge are sterile if divorced from moral purpose. I
know that the word moral makes many of us uneasy—
especially in the context of schools—but I use it with as
much force as I can summon, for in an age when faith in
the family or the church or even the country has disinte-
grated, the schools of America remain as the deepest
source of moral purpose—the center that must hold
against the anarchy which often threatens us. The respect
for truth, even in the face of mystery, is a perspective of
the sciences that must affect every thinking humanist—
and, of course, be shared by him. But moral criticism is a
distinct perspective of the humanist, whether or not it is
conveyed by someone who has prepared himself professionally as a scientist or critic of literature and the arts;
and it is a way of looking at the world that should touch
every student in an American school as a central strand in
the texture of his education. This is the humanistic perspective embedded in the study of the humanities, the
seed that waits to grow in everyone. The exploration of
literature, art, and music can never be contained within
the limitations of craft; for creation at the deepest level of
private self shares the mystery we associate with spirit
and transcendence. Students must touch this mystery—at
least they must know that it exists—or their education
lacks coherence; and educators must inform their work

with the sense of moral betterment, with the hope of improving the human being and his society, or their classes lack ultimate perspective and purpose.

We have lived through a period when many serious people have called into question the purpose of schools and have mocked them as prisons, or recorded their failures and limitations, and, in one form or another, repudiated the school system and recommended the establishment of alternate modes of education. But the failures of our schools are the failures of American society. Schools have been only as meaningful as the society they reflect. To make society more meaningful, schools need to go far beyond reflecting; they must be the lamp, not the mirror, and help to lead society. That finally was the noblest ambition of Open Admissions. For one brief moment, educators extended an invitation to those excluded from higher education and made them participants in the mutual estate of America. College faculties, who otherwise would never have considered these difficulties in language acquisition as their legitimate concerns, were forced to think about the problems posed by the new learners—and there is already important research and scholarship as a consequence. For a transitory moment, educators looked at a city in chaos—chaos caused largely by disaffected youths, roaming the streets and terrifying everyone, including themselves—and attempted to improve the quality of city life by improving the education of those who live there. What better purpose can an education have?

VIII

Open Admissions would have been a fact at The City College whether or not students stormed the buildings in 1969 and '70. An educationally better-prepared middle class was already emigrating from the public school system—the pool of those students had dramatically declined. Too few of us in the 1960s saw this shift of populations as the precursor to Open Admissions; too few of us, when we saw the need for Open Admissions, were willing to act upon our perceptions and plan for the vast attention underprepared students would need.

Although there was a commitment at The City College to the solutions of problems raised by language difficulties —a limited Center for Academic Skills was finally established and smaller programs sponsored—it was not sufficient; it did not carry the passion generated for the "elitist" programs in biomedicine, law, or performing arts; it foundered because language problems were so broad and deep and all-encompassing and existed within a college that was trying to accomplish everything at once. But language acquisition was basic to the development of a core curriculum and basic to any pre-professional or professional program and demanded Herculean efforts. The language problems were the roots of Open Admissions and would not allow anything else to grow until they were nurtured. We could have accomplished so much more at The City College, but, in my view, even with the greatest of efforts, these tangled roots of language difficulties cannot be nurtured sufficiently at a senior college where one expects students to acquire a liberal arts education and professional training within four years. Too much. Too fast. Too unrealistic. Too antihumanistic.

But in the same breath I would insist that college faculties—and especially those in programs of humanities, and social sciences, as well as of education—have the obligation in a democratic society to work with the faculties of elementary, junior and senior high schools, and community colleges.[3] They must train college tutors who will help teachers improve the language skills of younger students; they must develop summer programs in writing; they must participate in the retraining of teachers—ideas that are fully developed in the last chapter of this book. "A conjoint communicated experience" was Dewey's way of describing our democracy. Nowhere can the connection between the privileged and the poor, the well educated and the disadvantaged—the various elements that compose our conjoint communicated experience—be more dramatically achieved than through programs that promote the acquisition of language skills.

Open Admissions continues in practice, and the urban conditions that prompted this educational experiment in democracy remain to haunt us as memories of what we have thus far failed to achieve. Open Admissions will not

[3] At The City College, a campus high school has been established in which this opportunity presents itself most notably. The School of Education, under the strong leadership of the president and the dean, has worked toward the development of a comprehensive (i.e., non-selective) high school on the college campus. College faculty will work with high school teachers in creating the curriculum.

disappear; it will remain the fundamental reality of urban schools for the foreseeable future, and it must be implemented with common sense.

The life of the mind, so associated with the university, keeps us at a distance from the lives we actually lead. On the one hand, we often cling to the past as though afraid to make connections with the present. And because we have not discovered our own educational and moral center or established the bridge over which our students may walk, we sometimes become, on the other hand, victims of a momentary rage for relevance or ethnicity or vocationalism, like passive and defeated people who no longer believe in themselves.

It would be too easy to yield to the hollow feeling, so common in modern education, that all of these forces encourage our surrender to indifference, cynicism, negation, or sullen bitterness. It would be too easy, although at times one needs great courage and self-belief, a sense of humor, and a measure of luck. Some of the experiences I have just described were first printed, in an abbreviated version, in *Saturday Review*, February 4, 1978. I realize that my description of Open Admissions and some of my passing perceptions demand a program of action, and as someone who has been a teacher, scholar, and administrator, I offer my own recommendations in the final chapter. But I wish to place a parenthesis between the swift movement from description to solution—a moral parenthesis that is also a personal drama of some consequence. My record and my recommendations may then have a particular meaning, perhaps even a special truth because of what happened to me when I dared to publish an essay called "Open Admissions: A Confessional Meditation"— the core of the chapter you have just read. It will take you into the living storm of Open Admissions, of The City College, of the humanities in urban education. And it will reveal how difficult it can be to work toward the solutions of these problems I have outlined—even how difficult it is to attempt a simple statement of the problems, as one sees them personally.

Description is not enough; even recommended solutions, however cogent, are insufficient. At the root of our attempt to resolve these difficult issues lies our freedom to examine them openly and honestly, without fear of reprisal—our sense of intellectual security in the old standards of academic freedom and tolerance of dissent and independence of mind, without which any college is doomed, without which we will inevitably hesitate before we step forward. It is always safer to remain silent—and, for all of us, more dangerous. At the root of these problems is the sense of ourselves as educators.

Let me, then, present a case in point.

TWO

Publish and Perish

I

Sixteen months after I had written the essay, "Open Admissions: A Confessional Meditation"; five months from the day that *Saturday Review* had accepted it; one month after I had read the galleys; days after I had mentioned the article to members of the president's cabinet; on the final Thursday afternoon in January, when The City College campus was particularly crowded and my office was a network of bureaucratic details and phone calls, the chairman of the Asian studies department burst into my office with the article as it actually appeared in *Saturday Review.*

On the cover a thick dagger, dripping with blood, was plunged into the façade of a college building.

The publisher's title was "How to Kill a College: The Private Papers of a Campus Dean."

Opposite my text, swarms of headless students crowded

through the open doors of a college. A single dead tree provided the solitary landscape.

I phoned the editor of *Saturday Review*.

"What the hell have you done? That wasn't my title."

"We have the right to title."

"You didn't consult me. The piece is not about killing a college and it sure as hell is not from the private papers of a campus dean."

"We have the right to title. Do you think anyone would be interested in an article called 'Open Admissions: A Confessional Meditation'?"

"I can't believe this is happening."

Silence.

"I want a letter in the next issue, disavowing that title."

Silence. Then, "I'm sorry if this has caused you distress, Dean Gross; but we're in the magazine business, and we have to decide upon the best way to feature any given essay. You should know that we've already had very positive reactions to the piece. You should be pleased."

But I was not pleased—not with a cover and a title that, in my view, violated my intentions of description and analysis and understanding and compassion. This essay was the first chapter of a book about the humanities in urban education, not the opening scene of an academic melodrama. I felt abused by *Saturday Review*.

My colleagues in the administration and my friends on the faculty were equally indignant at the treatment of the essay, and they sent a flurry of letters to the editor—none of which was published. I sent my own letter of complaint, but it too was not acknowledged. In these first moments, I concentrated so intensely on the editors' sensational presentation of the piece that I minimized the inherent controversy of Open Admissions as a subject in itself. Already the essay was creating heated discussion on the campus, becoming the dramatic focus for many anxieties—declining enrollments, the ever-increasing commitment to remediation, the threat of faculty firings, the relationship of ethnicity to the curriculum, the role of affirmative action in hiring, the seemingly irreconcilable conflict between Open Admissions and academic excellence—that suppurated just below the surface of everyone's everyday behavior. For me, at the moment, it seemed extremely important to disavow that title and that cover—as if to clear the air for a discussion of the issues—and I tried to reach the young publisher who had recently bought the magazine from Norman Cousins; but for days he would not answer the telephone. Finally, he said, "We are in the business of selling magazines, Dean Gross," and concluded the matter, from his point of view, with a letter.

February 6, 1978

Dean Theodore L. Gross
The City College of New York
New York, New York 10031

Dear Dean Gross,

We are sorry the title and cover we chose for your article distressed you. The fact that you were not consulted on these matters, though, is nothing to apologize for.

We never consult our authors on title or illustrations because we believe that such consultation would not prove fruitful. Our job, as editors, is to present articles in the most arresting fashion possible, without alienating our readers. Recent increases in our circulation indicate that our readers endorse our decisions. I am willing to bet that our title and graphics will attract more readers to your article than a tamer title and graphics would have done.

If I felt that your proposed letter to the editor spoke to some issues raised by your piece, rather than to our internal methods, I would consider publishing it. But frankly, as it stands, I think it would be of marginal interest to our readers. Needless to say, I thought your piece was first rate. I think your misgivings about our handling of the piece are unjustified.

Sincerely,

Before I decided upon the action I would take, I alerted the president of the college to the change in title. He recommended I send a disclaimer to the faculty—and I took his advice—but the strong reactions to Open Admissions, voiced so often in the past, came to the surface once again. All of us, faculty and administration together, had struggled through these troubled years, grappling with the inevitable difficulties that arose from trying to provide the synthesis for a liberal arts education in the sudden context of Open Admissions. There had been so many crises: in the Basic Writing Program, where a large group of faculty had confronted the president in his conference room on a Saturday morning and demanded far greater resources for remediation; in the newly created Department of Asian Studies, where Maoist militants had taken over the president's office, insisting upon the imposition of their ideology; in the history department, where radicals and conservatives had torn at one another about standards, about the sort of history relevant to Open Admissions students, about who should or should not be chairman; in the biomedical program, where various legal suits—as crucial for us as *Bakke* was for California and the country—had involved conflicts in admissions for "minorities" (blacks, Hispanics, Asians) and "majorities" (Italians, Jews, and other white ethnics); in the frustrated faculty at large, where the publication of books and essays had borne funereal and apocalyptic titles that featured words like "death" and "end"—and now, as I regretted, "kill."

Again and again these incidents and confrontations and epistles to the world had charged the drama of Open Admissions and exerted extraordinary pressures upon the president and his administration. They had represented, no doubt, the intensity of administrative life everywhere in contemporary education—especially in the cities, especially in publicly funded institutions committed to Open Admissions—but the media exposure at The City College seemed more relentless than that of almost any other college in America. The college had, after all, this most distinguished history of academic excellence that was suddenly challenged by Open Admissions; it was located in Harlem (the "capital" of black America) and in New York (the center of communications in the world); and it had a large number of alumni who were journalists, sensitive to its problems and ready to report on them. I did not know the specific pressures that had been brought to bear upon the president in this particular case, but it was not hard to extrapolate from past experiences and to understand (if not appreciate) his first public reaction, which took the form of a letter to *Saturday Review*.

> On behalf of the entire City College community, I must express disappointment with the sensational and entirely inappropriate manner in which you featured Dean Theodore Gross's article. Furthermore, in your editorial introduction to the article, you demonstrate a shocking lack of understanding of the nature and history of open admissions by relating open admissions to the *Bakke* case. The former provides open access to some form of higher education to students of *all* ethnic groups, whereas the latter deals with the use of ethnic criteria in a limited-access situation. Moreover, you fail to point out that open admissions was introduced into the great state universities long before the "student rebellions" of the late Sixties.
>
> Your readers should also know that in matters of fact, particularly with regard to the creation of ethnic studies departments, Dean Gross's account is inaccurate. For example, the first ethnic studies department was created at City College in 1969—before the advent of open admissions—and not in 1971.[1] Dean Gross blames the decline of interest in the humanities on the creation of ethnic studies departments; enrollment in the humanities nationally declined from 9 percent to 5 percent during the period from 1969 to 1975, quite independent of the existence of ethnic studies departments.

[1] I had never claimed that the ethnic studies departments, discussed in 1971, were the first ones created but had written, "The dramatic moment came in the fall of 1971, at a large and raucous meeting of the Faculty Council, when *new* departments of ethnic studies were being considered."

In addition, Dean Gross's use of sexual, racial, and religious stereotypes is profoundly insulting to our student body and faculty. Contrast his statement "The blacks and Puerto Ricans and Asians arriving at the City College came from working-class families in which television and radio were the exclusive sources of information" with Charles Frankel's statement, in the December 1977 issue of *Change* magazine. "No one can deny that newspapers, radio, and television obsess the modern mind. They make virtues of glibness, of keeping up with the latest style in thought and feeling, of instant knowledge and instant judgment." Professor Frankel is trying to analyze a contemporary problem while Dean Gross is trying to find a scapegoat.

The editor had sent me the original version of this letter and invited me to reply. I was disappointed in the president's response, however much I may have understood the need for him to make it, however much I knew he felt the urgency to dissociate himself from almost any analysis of Open Admissions that was not entirely positive. I had expected him to discuss the matter with me privately, as we had so often in the past eight years, or to issue a joint statement; but all I heard of was his fury at my essay.

I continued to attend the round of meetings that constitute a dean's life: the Faculty Council of Liberal Arts and Science and the Faculty Senate of the entire college; the Curriculum Committee and the Dean's Council; the Review Committee of Deans and the Personnel/ Budget Committee of Chairpersons in the Humanities Division—twenty hours a week of meetings, minimum, where now I heard rumors upon rumors about the president's displeasure with the article. Several colleagues had assigned my essay for their basic writing courses; others came in to argue or agree with me; still others wrote articles in the campus newspapers, taking issue with my account. Through it all, I processed forms and supervised committees and carried on my deaconal responsibilities; but I knew that I could not control the dynamic series of events which had been unleashed—legal and journalistic and political—and I engaged an attorney to advise me.

The lawyer and I considered a suit against the magazine, but rejected the idea: too protracted, too publicly combative. Together we drafted a letter to *Saturday Review* that insisted the magazine print my rebuttal. It was hand-delivered to the publisher. Two weeks later, directly below the president's letter, my statement appeared.

> *Dean Gross* replies: The title and subtitle of my essay on open admissions—"How to Kill a College: The Private Papers of a Campus Dean"—were written by the editorial staff of *Saturday Review*, without my knowledge or approval. My own title was "Open Admissions: A Confessional Meditation," and there were no graphics in my manuscript.
>
> Any disinterested reader of my essay will see that I have not used sexual, racial, and religious stereotypes; and he will not need to know that I have spent the past 20 years doing research and writing my various books: *Dark Symphony: Negro Literature in America* (1968), *A Nation of Nations* (1971), and *The Literature of American Jews* (1973). I only regret that space did not allow me to amplify upon the Urban Educational Model at City College, which has

seen the creation of centers in biomedical education, legal education, and the performing arts, among other efforts, as well as to suggest solutions to the problems I describe. But my essay, as readers have realized, is the first chapter of a book on the humanities in urban education. The rest of the story will be told in subsequent chapters.[2]

From the moment I held the magazine in my hands and glared incredulously at the obscene cover and the cruel title so contrary to my own, I realized, quite consciously, that a political drama would take place which concentrated upon people and not upon issues. Out of my personal experiences, I had written what I hoped would be a thoughtful, sensitive account of Open Admissions—one of the most complicated, confusing, and important events in twentieth-century American education. I had struggled to go beyond the easy name-calling—liberal, conservative, radical, racist—which was so much a feature

[2] One of the incidental ironies of this academic tale is that the consequences of my having published in a commercial magazine altered my original intentions considerably. "The rest of the story" is still told in the last chapter, but rooted far more in the pragmatic than was my original plan—solutions now seem more imperative than theoretical discussion. The second chapter is obviously new. Thus the book I have written is different from the one I thought I would write. That book was to be about the future of the humanities in urban education, with separate chapters on foreign languages, philosophy, history, the performing and fine arts—an academic study to be read by academics—and the *Saturday Review* piece was chapter one: the background of Open Admissions, the study of language and literature, the relationship of professional education to the humanities. But when one considers higher education in these past twenty years—the student riots, the confusion over egalitarianism and excellence, the impact of professional education, the demands of ethnicity, the politics of education as they unfold in this chapter—perhaps my final result is more faithful to the felt experience of these years than a more conventional academic treatise would have been.

of this volatile subject and which automatically forced people into silence or evasion. But despite my attempt to compose a measured and balanced analysis—although obviously only partial—of Open Admissions at The City College, the essay had provoked extreme reactions for which I was not prepared.

During those short, snow-filled days of February, I often stared out of my office window at the students hurrying to classes along Convent Avenue, at the seventy-year-old college buildings around Jaspar Oval and beyond to a scarred cityscape that had always haunted my imagination: the tenements of Harlem, unchanged in all these years, bordering side streets up which so many immigrant children had climbed for an education—their passport out of poverty. These children of immigrants had walked by the people of Harlem as we the faculty had driven by them each day. The lives of the immigrant children had changed so dramatically in the space of a few years, but the lives of Harlem children seemed the same. Why? Had the cancer of racism infected the American system so deeply, so irrevocably?

And why—I would think, in the midst of these images and this tormenting question that informed the meaning and purpose of Open Admissions—why had I written the essay? Why had I sought to dig below questions that troubled all of us—liberals who wanted to open these academic doors but who recoiled at the everyday classroom experience? . . . Why? . . . Frustration at having had to fire thirty-three faculty, many of whom I had hired five years earlier, because of the financial bankruptcy of the university? Frustration at the chaos caused by special interest groups? At a breakdown in faculty morale? At the inability of intellectuals to solve their own problems as they complained so easily about everyone else in the culture at large? Or at watching literature and the arts surrender their future to more and more courses in basic writing? Frustration at so little progress despite my having worked closely with a president who in fact did have vision and purpose but who was pulled back inexorably by the many forces of a college and a city struggling to survive? . . .

And why had I published it? Because it told the truth? And what is the truth in so complex an educational enterprise as the City University of New York? Whose truth? . . . Why had I published this article? . . .

It was difficult to sort out motives, and most difficult to be honest with oneself, but I had watched, for more than ten years now, this large educational institution grow suddenly enormous with the promise of Open Admissions, then contract within two years and contract and contract and become paralyzed with ineffectuality despite the efforts of many extraordinary teachers and administrators, and at some point the sheer ineffectuality of the entire system somehow affected one's own sense of self, of professional dignity and purpose. One could make a separate peace, as so many of my friends had, and teach one's classes as well as one could, and say to hell with the bureaucracy—but one had one's own inevitable character, one had to try. . . . I had learned that "bureaucracy inhibits reform" and that "in mature bureaucracies self-doubt is minimal, for the forms of organizations work changes in the personalities of those who live within them." I knew now that one "effect of bureaucracy is to make bureaucrats"—and breaking through the bureaucracy was certainly one strong reason for my trying. . . .

The university could not seem to meet the needs of the new learners and shape an education that brought them into the middle class. In the room where the deans convened, everyone studied flow charts and data and bickered with one another about the few dollars remaining after salaries had been paid and heat and electricity bills settled. The talent in the room was extraordinary, but so often reduced to reacting defensively against city and state legislators who refused to concede the cost-effectiveness of the college. . . . A confusion of motives, a confusion of intentions. . . . If you write about the problems (I told myself) and define them perceptively, you can move toward a solution and alter, a little, the nature of the bureaucracy; otherwise, the endless memos will meet no more than a momentary crisis, and the promise of Open Admissions will fade until the City University becomes like too many other American schools in which "poor children become poor adults" and "schools are not great democratic engines for identifying talent and matching it with opportunity." . . . But you never know your next budget, Ted (someone complained years ago, in the talented room), or you're constrained by a mayor who withholds support (someone else reminded me), so how can anyone plan a future that makes sense?

II

During the weeks following the publication of the essay, I heard that the president was writing an extended personal response to me. Each day the letter was due; each day it did not come. But his initial reaction set the stage for his staff and close associates. They attacked me for criticizing Open Admissions, for saying the college was dead, for going public at all, for not waiting until all the evidence was in, for not realizing a student could learn as much from Langston Hughes as from Shakespeare, for claiming the furniture in the lounge was only "makeshift," for using my position as dean, for appealing to the forces of bigotry, for being bigoted myself, for opening up old wounds and even for daring to tell the truth—storm signals before the inevitable hurricane of presidential anger.

Across the campus, this incident was only one of many, as we taught our classes and students hurried from them to work so that they could support themselves while studying—the old City College ethic. The business of an urban college went on, despite any momentary crisis, its pitch and beat most vividly caught in the headlines of the campus newspapers during February and March of 1978: "City College facing a $1 million budget cut. . . . [Vice-president] indicted on larceny charge. . . . Enrollment declines for seventh time. . . . $500,000 college renovation to begin in spring. . . . Snack bar closes: natural foods saved. . . . Woman raped in afternoon. . . . Benson [a jazz singer] shows he's greatest. . . . Beavers [the college basketball team] ready to trip Hunter and Cunys. . . . Legal Aid Center awaits allocation. . . . College majority blasts press illiteracy charge. . . . Library to show French films. . . . English department writing awards. . . . Forum on South Africa. . . . New pre-med program scheduled. . . . Success of SEEK? You Decide. . . . President calls for commission to study problems with CLAS [College of Liberal Arts and Science]. . . . Freshman enrollment may stabilize. . . . Skills test denounced at open PAC [Policy Advisory Committee to the president] meeting. . . . Home again, Baldwin lectures at college. . . . College won't close if transit strikes. . . ."

. . . And the classes ran from eight in the morning until eleven at night, fifteen thousand students, eight hundred faculty moving across this asphalt campus. . . .

Those in the administration who had privately expressed admiration for my essay fell quickly into silence and put nothing in writing. Others who represented specific constituencies at the college played out their roles, like actors in a Pirandello play: the head of Women's Studies, of SEEK, of Public Relations, of the students; the provost; the ombudsman for the faculty. All political, all predictable, all understandable—but still depressing. An institutional mask concealed the human being who wore it so that he or she was little more than an actor with a prepared text. The inversion of Forster's famous line summarized my sense of personal betrayal— each of them would sacrifice a colleague, even a friend, for the institution he/she needed. I had been more or less friendly with them all—some former teachers of literature and psychology—and knew how analytical and fair-minded they could be when not personally threatened; but now they felt obliged to attack me in the name of Womanhood, Blackness, Students—in the name of the Institution—with copies of their letters for appropriate colleagues and almost always for the president. . . . At the time, I was resentful; but even then I could read the fear in their letters. Those near the president had no choice. . . . And these letters as well as whatever private meetings and private phone calls commanded the president's attention must have exerted enormous influence on him. . . .

Fortunately—for my sense of perspective, at least—there were phone calls at all hours of the day and night, from colleagues who confirmed the experience I had described, who agreed or argued with my conclusions, who fought my ideas, who saw the essay as an essay and not merely as a public relations document. And there were friends of both the president and me who spent long hours analyzing the president's behavior, suggesting strategy to me, trying to heal this wound before it grew worse, and to restore a relationship, a friendship, that had gone beyond the institution. Each day colleagues came into my office to extend a sympathetic word or to seek a wider discussion of the issues—a symposium, a conference, a dialogue—or to lament the unfortunate truth of what I had said.

Letters continued to arrive from across the country

that praised me for my courage and integrity, my willingness to say what needed to be said—letters from the well known and from the obscure that made me realize how deeply self-protective my own administration was. At the same time, I now knew—more intensely than ever before —how impossibly difficult it was for any college official to speak forthrightly: the social and political and religious and racial and economic and sexual and historical forces ran through one's head, warning of this or that consequence, before one could make the simplest statement. One had a crude choice in the bureaucracy of modern education—to survive or not to survive—and too often the university seemed little more than a business that marketed culture as entertainment and degrees as social revenue; or, even more dangerously, it had come to resemble in so many places a public relations firm where academic freedom and dissent and independence of mind cowered before the importance of the corporate image.

I knew that something far deeper was at stake than the private (and finally superficial) strains between a president and his dean—I knew this from the response to my essay. I had touched a nerve so raw in classroom teachers on every level of education, it provoked an outcry for which I was scarcely prepared. Across the country, it appeared, so many teachers of humanities felt that they had met the Waterloo of their personal careers. They had not entered teaching for the money—so they told me—and scarcely for prestige and surely not to implement any grand social or educational vision. The original purpose of most was really very modest. They had wished to share with young people their own love of reading, of music and theater and art. But now too few students lingered after class—too many avoided school—too many were bored. So many reasons, so often cited in those letters that I received: technology, television, narcissism, hedonism, urban pathology—the list seemed endless. The student wanted *this* moment, *that* future, an instant gratification which made the humanities—rooted in the past, often marked by doubt and ambiguity and even negation—incompatible with his assertive, optimistic spirit. Those teachers who wrote me were idealists fighting their own inclination toward cynicism, negation, and negligence; but the generation gap—a book-oriented faculty facing a visually saturated student body—was more profound than ever before in human history; and the teachers were confused and in despair, and they wondered how the humanities could survive in their classrooms. . . .

At that time—in February and March of '78—these letters confirmed my own views of the state of the humanities at The City College and in the city colleges of this country. The teachers did not ask for panaceas, or rhetorical denunciations, or easy lamentations, or radical alternatives to the reality of their teaching. Nor could they respond any longer to simple solutions—they knew that the problems confronted by humanists went beyond their own classrooms. But they were grateful for a statement that confirmed the validity of their profession. And I was grateful for their sympathetic response. These teachers were scattered across America and were responding to my writing as writing and to my ideas as ideas. I worked at The City College and had to deal with the dailiness of my life there—and that had to do as much with the politics and business and bureaucracy of education as with education itself. Each day began to feel like another round in a prize fight that would never end and that carried with it a truth Hemingway had discovered years ago: the winner takes nothing.

The phone rang—at every hour of the day and night and in the darkness at noon. . . . A writer/teacher: "Brilliant, Ted, but it won't help the college. Still, we took an oath when we came into this profession—to tell the truth. Don't let the stuffed dummies get you. Damn the torpedoes." . . . A black woman, who had earned her Ph.D. in English literature spoke to me with passion: "I grew up in separate but equal schools and hated them. Never believed in black studies. Don't listen to the name-calling, Ted—it's all politics and posturing. They know you're right, Ted, but they can't admit it publicly—not yet." . . . A physicist who sat next to me at the Review Committee of Deans could not believe that *Saturday Review* would sensationalize anyone's writing to this extent: "Was that your title, Ted, or theirs? Didn't they even consult you?" . . . A professor of elementary education to the president directly: "I too work in Shepard and I see the students, representing New York's racial and cultural diversity, as they pass through the halls. I am always overhearing as I wait in line in the cafeteria bits and pieces of discussion on big and intellectual issues. I am endlessly attracted by the student's [*sic*] alert, lively, and purposeful demeanor. . . . After such an attack, it can in no sense be appropriate that Dean Gross continue in the role of dean." . . .

And on and on and on: a truthful record; the mediocre fear excellence; the best account yet of Open Admissions; you're stating the obvious—everyone out of New York knows it but only those outside that immediate presidential circle can afford to admit it; integrity; group libel; eloquent; indiscreet. . . . A black militant group met with the president to express their dismay and to ask for my resignation. Influential figures in New York education warned the president to show restraint, for fear of his being accused of abridging academic freedom and of being, in fact, intolerant of dissent—he was overreacting to a complex critical essay that many, many people thought represented an accurate picture of Open Admissions.

Each day the president's letter was due, each day it did not come. Someone said he even saw him scribbling it between acts at the Metropolitan Opera. The letter had become an obsessive act, an absurd quixotic gesture—but at the time it held no sense of absurdity for the president and me. Apart from his private views on the matter, the political pressures must have forced a direct, public reply and compelled him to make it clear that he wished to be dissociated from me. From my point of view, I knew that his letter marked the direction this affair would take. It came—three weeks after the article had been published—a five-page, single-spaced, open letter, sent to the college community; sent to alumni; sent to wealthy and influential friends of the college; sent, it seemed, to everyone.

February 21, 1978

Dean Theodore L. Gross
Dean of Humanities
The City College

Dear Ted:

I have now had an opportunity to study your article entitled "How to Kill a College: The Private Papers of a Campus Dean" which appeared in the February 4, 1978 issue of the *Saturday Review*. The character and timing of your article require an official public response from me as President of City College.

I find it hard to believe that the Dean of Humanities would publish an article so deeply offensive to our students and faculty and so devoid of understanding of the progress made in the past few years at City College. Apart from the change in title and graphics, for which you disavow responsibility or knowledge, you nevertheless authorized the publication of an article in the text of which you flaunted your position as Dean of Humanities, thereby cooperating with the *Saturday Review*'s effort to gain readership for the article by capitalizing on your administrative rank at the College.

Then a detailed and rather tedious analysis of my essay that concluded with an effort at public relations:

Nonetheless, I can assure the college community that the damage resulting from your article will be contained and that City College will continue to demonstrate for generations to come, as it has through its 131-year history, that educational opportunity and academic excellence cannot only coexist but be mutually reinforcing—with great benefits to our pluralistic society.

Sincerely yours,

This letter led to scores of others, in and out of the campus newspapers, sent to me privately and printed publicly—an unfortunate incident was now becoming a *cause célèbre*, a delicious row between a dean and his president. Up to the moment of publication, as one reporter put it, I was "a deservedly favored administrator" in the president's "cabinet"; now I was *persona non grata*. This was the stuff of drama, carrying (as this same journalist, a venerable administrator and professor of English emeritus, reminded his readers) a powerful theme: the "Orwellian danger to freedom of speech and intellectual honesty."

A reporter from the *Daily News*, who was a student at the college, called me at 11:00 P.M.: "Are you resigning? . . . What was your reaction to the president's letter? Did you expect it to be so long—so bitter? . . . What do you mean you won't respond? I'm running the story anyway so you'd better give me your side. . . . Of course there's a story. You know there's a story. . . ." I refused to answer his questions, and he was angry, so the story that ran in the New York *Daily News* was less favorable than it might have been.

Rap at Open Admissions
Puts CCNY Dean in Soup

A City College dean is under fire from colleagues as a result of a magazine article in which he blasted

the City University educational [*sic*] system and its
open-admissions policy.

The article by Dean of Humanities Theodore
Gross was entitled, "How to Kill a College—the Private Papers of a Campus Dean." It appeared in the
February 4 issue of *Saturday Review* and immediately set off an academic furor.

It described the impact of the open-admissions
policy, which guarantees a place in the City University system to any New York City high school graduate who wants a college education.

Under this policy, Gross wrote, "minorities, including now impatient women, used affirmative action to leap into positions of power." He said that
ethnic studies programs, created under open admissions, led to "courses that could only encourage militant separatism."

The article also contended that a normal black
child, reared in a normal family, "will become abnormal on the slightest contact with the white world"
[*sic*].

Angry faculty members and administrators met
with [the] City College President . . . last week to
denounce the article. Some faculty members supported Gross; others demanded his ouster.

"He should resign," said [the] Black Studies
Chairman . . . who called the article "spurious, vicious, almost pathological."

I was livid with anger. My essay had criticized a course
description which stated that a normal black child, reared
in a normal family, "will become abnormal on the
slightest contact with the white world"; I had noted it as
a dangerous example of how the races could be only fur-

ther separated, and I had deplored the dangerous tendency of writing apocalyptic prose for a college course description.

I confronted the student journalist. He smiled sheep-
ishly and said that, in rushing to meet his deadline, a
line had been left out but that the article was corrected
in a later edition. "See—" and he showed me the altered
copy. "For example, in the article, Gross cited an ethnic
studies course description in 1971 which contended that a
normal black child, reared in a normal family, 'will become abnormal on the slightest contact with the white
world.'" I wanted to write a letter of correction to the editor, but my lawyer told me to forget it—"don't react, not
yet." Still the original copy was picked up by the television station that the *News* operated and I could only listen to the announcer with a sense of impotent rage—then
listen later to my sixteen-year-old daughter tell me that
her friends had heard her father mentioned on the
radio. . . .

Like forces that gather to warn of an incipient tornado,
the winds of this conflict darkened, thickened, and moved
to engulf me. I blessed the heavy snow that canceled
classes and blanketed the campus. Perhaps the winds
would suddenly dissipate and blow away: City College
entertained at least a monthly crisis, and one usually canceled out the other. Perhaps another issue would eclipse
me. I decided not to answer the president's letter, for, as
so many faculty told me, it revealed itself as an *ad ho-
minem* attack on a man's character for his ideas. I tried to
believe my friends, who kept assuring me that "this too

will pass"—although one friend reminded me that these words were from an Anglo-Saxon poem, "Deor," and really read, "This too *may* pass." Then George Will and Andrew Greeley, syndicated, conservative columnists, praised the essay and used my arguments to support their own historical opposition to Open Admissions. As Will wrote, "One legacy of the turmoil of the late 1960s and 1970s is a literature of political remorse, recollections of lessons learned at great cost to individuals and institutions. . . . One blessing of New York's financial crisis is that open admissions has been scrapped. That policy, promising a real college education for everyone, was not just a dream born out of season. It was a dream for which there can be no season." A new rash of letters was sent to the president and me. A campus newspaper ran the entire essay and that, in turn, generated local reactions—"a courageous public statement"; "the elitist's liberal way"; "lucid, searching, and essentially true"; "ahistorical"; "in the splendid humanistic tradition of self-criticism."

In the midst of these personal events, a larger drama was developing within the university itself: the implementation of a two-year skills test. Authorities from the central office at The City University of New York were insisting that students demonstrate ninth grade competence in writing and mathematics before they be allowed to continue beyond their sophomore year in college. Local campuses, always jealous of their own autonomy, objected for a variety of technical reasons. The real opposition, however, came from militant students who claimed racism, exclusion, and imperialism—they feared that the university was using the test as an excuse to keep them out of college simply to save money—and for a moment it seemed as though we had returned to 1969, when the same language was used to discuss Open Admissions. It was difficult to speak of the matter rationally and smart people—that is, people who manage to survive—did not speak at all or spoke with the blurry qualifications of academic jargon. Indeed, at one forum on the City College campus, the president grew so furious at certain bellicose students, who had accused him of not opposing the tests with sufficient vigor, that he stormed out of the meeting. "When the going gets tough, the tough get going," the student reporters mocked him, and quoted his reason for leaving: "I think the students are always directing questions at me which aren't relevant." The provost was left to make the final statement: "No one is going to get a City College diploma unless they [sic] meet our level of competency."

At the same time, the New York *Post,* quite independently, ran a scurrilous three-part series on illiteracy at The City College:

> *Illiterates in the thousands passing through City*
> Thousands of functionally illiterate students—many with only a third-grade understanding of English—are being pushed through City College under an open admissions policy that has proven a cruel hoax on the minorities it was intended to help. . . .
>
> *City College: Scandal of the "failures" who graduate*
> Each year more than $16 million in federal and state tuition aid pours into the hands of City College stu-

dents—money that is intended to bring hope and opportunity, but which far too often leads only to disillusionment. . . .

Illiterate students scandal: CCNY profs blame prexy
The controversy over open admissions and the internal politics that surround it have left the faculty at City College bitter and divided. . . .

The series was filled with unsubstantiated statements of this kind and with distortions and misinformation, supported by quotations from a small group of disaffected faculty who resented the president and his administration. Yellow journalism of the worst sort, but real enough to create a panic in those who are dependent on city and state officials for their budget. A fellow dean smiled at me and said, "You're off the hook, Gross; here's the crisis that will obscure you"; but that would not prove to be true. I was momentarily forgotten.

For one desperate week everyone in the administration had different suggestions of how to respond to the New York *Post*. Data were gathered; arguments marshaled; a press release distributed, which began, "Vicious slander—" A rebuttal from the president was issued in the form of an open letter to "the Students, Faculty, and Alumni of City College," and finally a statement of defense was spread across a page in the New York *Post*, with facts and figures on how successful the educational process was at City College. It began and ended with these paragraphs:

The current series of New York *Post* articles on City College charges that thousands of functionally illiterate students are being pushed through the College to keep up an enrollment in order to protect faculty and administrative jobs because budget is determined by level of enrollment. . . . Apart from the small group of notorious faculty malcontents at City College, the quality of the faculty at the College has never been higher: whether in the traditional disciplines or in the new centers of biomedicine, legal studies or performing arts.

City College will continue to be an institution of quality and service to its students, its City, and its Nation.

The scandal itself passed in a week, but the issue of the skills test remained. For the militant students I became a visible, representative, and handy target of all those forces that were visiting standards upon them—a scapegoat, in an instant, for a demonstration, when no other scapegoat existed.

DEAN GROSS—YOU CAN'T HIDE
MEET DEAN GROSS FACE TO FACE

RALLY IN FRONT OF HIS OFFICE ON MARCH 13 12 P.M. SHEPARD HALL HIS ARTICLE IN SATURDAY REVIEW (REPRINTED IN THE LAST OP) ARTICULATES HIS VIEW OF *US* CITY COLLEGE STUDENTS. IT IS THE SAME AS THE VIEW EXPRESSED IN THE POST'S ARTICLES—TO LAY BASIS FOR FURTHER ATTACKS ON MINORITY STUDENTS AND THEIR EDUCATION, SUCH AS THE *TWO YEAR TEST*.
JOIN US ON MONDAY—12 NOON AT OUR MEETING WITH HIM (HE HAS AGREED TO MEET WITH STUDENTS).

Revolutionary Student Brigade   Committee Against Racism
Concerned Students   Student Christian Fellowship
Revolutionary Youth League   Day Student Senate
   Greek Students

On the previous Wednesday, March 8, before this flier was distributed and the "rally" organized, the students (none of whom knew me personally) had congregated in Shepard Hall and marched throughout Lincoln Corridor, carrying placards and chanting, "Gross, you liar, we'll set your ass on fire." Many of the students were from an organization called the Revolutionary Student Brigade and did not even attend City College; others were leaders of marginal militant groups that most of the student body—conservative in the seventies, concerned with their courses and with earning enough money to support themselves—avoided.

At the time of the march, I was at a meeting.

> 50 students [as the college newspaper reported] swarmed into the office of Dean Theodore Gross (Humanities) on Wednesday [March 8] demanding his resignation. The students were among 150 who rallied for two hours on North Campus in protest over recent attacks on the College by both Gross and The New York Post.
>
> The protesters assembled at 1:00 P.M., in front of Shepard Hall, gathering forces for the march inside to Gross' first floor office, where they pounded on his doors demanding entry. After Gross' secretary opened the door to announce that Gross was not there, the students moved into the office.
>
> "I heard the noise in the corridor and locked the doors. But then I let them in because I thought they'd break the glass," said . . . the secretary. "I said they were infringing upon my rights, but that didn't seem to mean anything to them."
>
> Although [the secretary] refused to discuss Gross'

whereabouts except to say "I know where he is," she, without consulting Gross, granted the protesters an interview with him next Monday. Upon obtaining the appointment, the protesters left. [The] director of security then stationed himself inside Gross' office and relocked the doors.

Reached on Thursday, Gross said he was "surprised" about the march but said he would meet with the students Monday [March 13].

"I will talk to anybody so long as the discussion is rational," he said. However, when asked what he would say to the students if they asked him to resign, Gross answered, "No comment."

Then the article continued to describe the behavior of two administrators close to the president.

Administrators to the Scene

Word of the march to Gross' office traveled quickly, bringing several College administrators to the scene, including [the] vice provost for student affairs and [the] acting dean for community relations.

"I favor any kind of student protest against something which has done extreme harm to the College," said [the Vice-provost for Student Affairs], in an interview before the rally. "My feelings about the rally haven't changed. The students left with no problems," she later said.

"The students have been taking a lot of clobbering lately. I think the rally is terrific as long as it remains peaceful," said [the Acting Dean for Community Relations].

One of the militant leaders claimed success, even though I had not yet uttered a word to anyone. "The rally proved students were serious," he was quoted as saying, for the president "will now have to relieve Gross of his position as dean. If [the president] fires him as dean, Gross will not stay."

But another student, a bystander, seemed less determined: "I don't even know what they're screaming about. They are making a whole lot of noise and expect everybody to understand their arguments. . . . How can I understand their arguments when they hold such a confusing and disorganized event like this?"

The reported behavior of the Vice-provost for Student Affairs and the Acting Dean for Community Relations—what was immediately identified as incitements to riot—triggered sharp reaction from faculty who had thus far remained silent. Clear-headed responses from people I did not know suggested that this community of teachers and students—this City College of New York—was still fundamentally healthy, despite the egregious behavior of individual administrators or of a handful of student extremists or even of a president who remained silent throughout these demonstrations. One letter, addressed to the two administrators, summarized the feelings of many faculty.

> Dear Colleagues,
>
> *The Campus* for March 10 reports that you expressed approval of the "rally" [on March 8] in Dean Gross's office. If this report is correct, it is outrageous that a college professor or administrator would condone deliberate, organized harassment of a colleague because of his opinions. Apparently you subscribe to

the all-too-common doctrine that evil becomes good when it is labeled "left," "black," "third world," etc. The principal purpose of the demonstrators was not to express opinions of their own—an obscene chant has no cognitive content—but to discourage expression by others. Dramatic incidents like this are only the tip of an iceberg. The bulk of it is the articles that are not written, the lectures that are not given, the research that is not undertaken because silence is the way to avoid trouble.

Academic freedom in the United States has historically been the shield of the left against those who yearn to purge the colleges of radicals, subversives, etc. Now it seems that some segments of the left feel strong enough to attempt their own purges, on the cynical premise that "when you are stronger, we deny you freedom because that is our principle." They should recognize that the more they chip away at freedom today, the less of it will be there to protect them the next time.

Sincerely yours,

The meeting with the militant students was set for the following Monday, March 13, at noon, when I would discuss the entire matter with them.

III

On Monday morning, at eleven-thirty, the captain of Security, a large man who had a reputation for grace under pressure, came into my office with two guards; they would be with me all day. Their presence made the office look like a military station, their walkie-talkies suggested a battlefront. The Vice-provost for Student Affairs phoned my secretary to ask if I wanted her present—no. At eleven-fifty, the Provost for Academic Affairs moved quickly into my office. Her face was pale.

"Do you want me to stay?"

"It won't be necessary."

She left more quickly than she had come.

Moments later, one of her staff assistants—tall, heavyset—came in to represent official administrative protection. Soon we could hear the student leaders marching outside, clapping in the corridors, using a megaphone, searching for a crowd, chanting words that were unclear to me as I stood near my desk, waiting. They had spread fliers on the tables in the cafeteria below, urging others to attend the confrontation, trying to stir up a mild revolution; but their efforts were largely unsuccessful as students ran off to classes or continued eating their lunch. For a moment it seemed as though this unfocused demonstration might never take place for lack of support. But a few diehards resumed the chant and repeated my name: "Gross, Gross, you liar, we'll set your ass on fire." On the windows of my office someone had slapped a sign: "Dean Gross . . . You better think about where you are going next! Retract! Resign!" And after several minutes of marching, there were enough militants as well as curious onlookers to qualify for a demonstration.

The captain of Security returned from speaking to the students.

"How do you want to work this? Some of them are not even our students."

"Who are they?"

"The Revolutionary Student Brigade. They come from everywhere to support local demonstrations."

I could scarcely think.

"Let me see ten at a time until I've seen them all. I won't talk to a mob—there'll only be shouting."

A moment after he had relayed my message to them in Lincoln Corridor, I could hear the chant clearly and loudly: "See, he lied, he lied. He said he'd meet us and now he chickens out. He wants to divide and conquer. . . . Gross, Gross, you liar. We'll set your ass on fire."

The captain returned.

"They insist on coming in a group."

I nodded. . . . "Let them in."

The doors were flung open and the students came in slowly, circling the room, the few leaders looking at me with great suspicion and distrust, the majority drawn into the office by wonder and anticipation. Fifty, seventy students—I lost count as they stood on the leather couch and on the chairs and squeezed together on the limited floor space in the room. They encircled me. They pressed close. On my left, the captain of Security; on my right, the administration's representative; outside the office, a cluster of sympathetic faculty members, fearing what might happen; off in another building a busy president—busy with other matters; and in my office, suddenly grown very small, the students.

One of their leaders, an angry white girl from the Revolutionary Brigade who was not a student, was the spokesperson. A small, thin Hispanic girl—she could not have been more than eighteen, could not have weighed more than eighty pounds—was the moderator: she seemed to be a student. She would designate who could speak, who could not, and it was clear that the bitterness in her eyes would not be even mildly satisfied until she had wreaked vengeance upon me, her unknown enemy. I leaned against the back of my desk, fixing my face into a frozen mask. After a moment, I realized that there were really no more than five or six demonstrators—the rest were onlookers, uncertain of why they were even here.

At first the voices of the leaders were angry: "I think most of us are here because we're concerned that you wrote about us in this national newspaper. [i.e., *Saturday Review*] . . . Will you retract what you said? . . . We want to know if you'll retract that article."

"You've got the wrong scapegoat. I've spent the last twenty years of my life at this college trying to set up writing programs for black and Hispanic and Asian students . . . teaching . . . writing books on ethnicity. . . . I care." But this defensive posture carried no authority with them—my past was my own and belonged to no one else—and I soon became irritated at myself for being self-defensive. "I believe in Open Admissions very deeply. That doesn't mean I believe in the way it was implemented."

The Puerto Rican girl glared at me.

"I'm not stupid, you know. I may be from another country and can't speak English good, but I'm not stupid. You embarrassed me."

We looked at each other for an extended moment, but I knew I could not answer her—not in the midst of this public drama—and I let her revile me before those few friends of hers who stood nearby.

"Retract or resign," echoed her friends.

"I'm not resigning or retracting. There's no reason to resign for writing an article. What have we come to? Is that the kind of college you want to attend? Do you want someone punished for what he publishes?"

"Do you believe in the Skills test?"

"I—"

"Don't snow us. Do you believe in it?"

"Yes."

"See—see. . . . What did I tell you?"

One student, disgusted with the proceedings, stepped forward. "Listen, Gross, you've got to retract what you said or we're not going to let up. We're going to force your resignation—hear?"

"You say in that essay that most of us need basic skills. You say we shouldn't be in college."

"I didn't say that."

"You say we're not good enough."

"I didn't say that."

"You say we have only a third-grade knowledge of English."

"That's the *Post* article," someone corrected.

"Well, we ain't illiterates passing through City College."

"That's the New York *Post* article—this man didn't write that."

"You—"

"I—"

"We—"

The militant leaders became increasingly impatient as they sensed that most of the students were growing far less sympathetic and were now uneasy with this confrontation, uncertain of what was true, untrue, right or wrong, and irritated that they had been manipulated into coming at all. The militants kept trying to bring the discussion back to the argument, back to the point they had come to make, as a photographer kept clicking and clicking away. They tried to sustain their anger, but other students began to disagree quite openly with them, out of a sense of fairness, and the chemistry in the room altered perceptibly until my office became a different kind of space—a more familiar kind of space—a classroom. As I talked, the students grew more generous to my situation and refused to be intimidated by the militants, accusing them of being unreasonable, saying they were unfair, moving away in fatigue or in a desire to leave for classes or home or work. Weariness was setting in, dispersal only a moment away.

Then something remarkable happened—a teacher's dream of what might happen in a classroom. As the five or six angry students, afraid that I might elude their grasp, crowded me and moved closer and demanded retraction or resignation, a young woman emerged from somewhere in that room. Thin. Black. Glasses. With a coat that touched her ankles. A thirty-year-old mother who was in the course on modern American literature I was teaching that semester. One of my finest students—a lightning rod for the other students. She was studying at The City College for a master's degree in creative writing. She seemed to be one of those people who convert order from chaos, sense from sentimentality, compassion from cruelty; and she bore herself with great but simple dignity.

"Have you read the essay?" she asked the Puerto Rican girl.

"No—but *he* told me it was no good. *He* told me."

She turned to the leader of the Revolutionary Brigade. "Have you read this?"

"Part of it. But I'm gonna read the rest—"

"Then how can you criticize this man? How can you attack him?"

I could feel a cloud lift from the room. The other students now stirred self-consciously, murmured to one another, and criticized the militants openly.

One young man came up to me. "You're being screwed."

Someone turned to the leader of the Revolutionary Brigade. "You're not interested in Gross. You just want a scapegoat."

"How can you scream at him?" this black woman went on, with deliberation. "This is a college. You wouldn't do this in a classroom."

The two angry white leaders—one a student, one not even a student—were afraid of her. The Hispanic girl stood there, puzzled. A black man, who had been most aggressive toward me, was furious with her, and took a step forward.

"Where you coming from? You know this man? He set you up?" Slowly, deliberately: "Where are you coming from?"

She returned his glare and did not pause.

"I'm coming from myself."

It was already three o'clock in the afternoon and students had begun to leave. Some lingered to discuss the issues with the black woman, trying to persuade her that they were sincere. They had read the essay or would read it; they *were* being fair; they *were* trying to understand.

"I do believe we need standards. I know that I need help."

And I felt empty, hurt that they were hurt, and sad if I had misunderstood, and troubled most deeply by that same Puerto Rican girl who still looked at me—it was now three-thirty in the afternoon—with a bitterness in her eyes that went far beyond me and had to reflect some hatred of a school system or culture or set of personal circumstances that had placed her here, before me, as a leader of a demonstration fast disintegrating and leaving her alone. And it was clear that this was also true for her friend, and for the angry black student, if not for those outsiders from the Revolutionary Brigade who had a political agenda on which I was simply a usable item. The City College students wanted help—now—and they felt trapped in their own poor preparation, resentful, defensive, too old for this confrontation.

After the students had drifted away and only a few remained, together with those sympathetic faculty and administrators who had waited outside my office, the phone rang.

"This is the New York *Post*."

"Oh. . . ." A journalist identified himself—the same man who had smeared the college in those impressionistic, inaccurate articles.

"I understand there was a student demonstration in your office today."

"Yes."

"Sixty—seventy characters."

"The students and I had a meeting."

"Oh no. I understand you had quite a little demonstration. Don't you want *your* side of the story told. . . . I'm going to do a piece anyway, you know. . . . Were they violent?"

"Look—"

"Did they bring the Brigade with them?"

"I have nothing to say."

"Let me leave you my number, in case you want to call before I publish this story."

But he never published a word.

Four days later, the article appeared in *The Campus*—"Gross' resignation demanded by students." Seven pictures were framed in separate panels, revealing me in various positions before the students—defensive, accusatory, dejected, with one panel featuring the cover of *Saturday Review*. And it ended: "After about an hour and a half of questioning, the students began to debate the Gross article among themselves, leaving the Dean sitting dejectedly on his desk."

IV

In the days that followed the student demonstration, I lived in a schizophrenic world. Each day letters would come from across the country, praising the essay—it was balanced and courageous and perceptive and sensitive; someone needed finally to tell the truth about what was happening. Each day I would walk through Lincoln Corridor like Dr. Stockmann in *An Enemy of the People*, leaving my office only to attend an obligatory meeting. I continued to conduct interviews and meetings that concerned my division of humanities—new appointments, a grant proposal, a prospective conference on mass communications, the status of our performing arts programs, consultations with chairpersons and faculty and students —but I lost enthusiasm before the uncertain future that awaited me. I was a dean, but (for the first time in eight years) the president did not communicate with me, and the provost began to send letters that contained strange sentences of reprobation. Was a file being kept? A black book? I began to take my own notes, but the tension was too great, too often, and I neglected to write down every detail. . . .

It seemed especially important during these dark days to work quite regularly, to be absolutely punctual, to carry on so that the reality of what was whirling round me would not become obsessive. But at the same time, my analysis of Open Admissions had provoked renewed discussion of a subject that seemed particularly com-

pelling to Americans everywhere, at every level of education. The subject elicited an intense reaction that went
far beyond the liberal's support of the underprivileged,
the conservative's hatred of a breakdown in "standards":
it went to the root of being American, of being generous
and open and self-improving and yet heroic, intellectual,
and idealistic; of being active and yet thoughtful; of
being as pragmatic as Ben Franklin and as idealistic as
Jonathan Edwards. There was no other way to explain the
visceral response to Open Admissions whenever one met
the middle class or the economically elite, almost anyone
who had hitched his wagon to an American star; it was an
educational experiment so fundamentally in the American
grain that no one championed or denounced it without
making the argument personal. For in everybody's family
there was an Open Admissions student—usually a highly
motivated, idealistic relative—a grandfather, an uncle, a
cousin who once struggled with English as a second language and wanted admission into our mutual estate. And
so I found myself called upon to speak about the experiment of Open Admissions that troubled so many people.

The phone rang on the morning of March 28.

"Would you appear on the ABC program 'Report Card'
—about your article?"

I had to set the record straight.

"Yes," I said.

"Would you lecture at our adult center? . . . Would
you lecture at the conference of high school chairpersons? . . . Would you speak on the Humanities in a
Technological Age? The Humanities in Our Time? The

Reason for the Decline of the Humanities? The Humanities and the Human Experience in the Contemporary World? The Pursuit of Excellence at a Time of Broadening Access to Higher Education? Open Admissions and a Liberal Arts Education? In the Bronx, in Chattanooga, in Houston, in Kansas City, in Vienna. . . ."

Yes, yes, yes, yes.

The lecture "Open Admissions and a Liberal Arts Education" was to be given at the Rockefeller Foundation as part of a day-long conference to which key educators from across the country had been invited. Open Admissions had officially ended in 1976, with the imposition of tuition, and there was the sense that the six-year experiment needed the definition and description of historical perspective by not only the people who had helped to shape it but also by those who had watched its development with great professional interest. Benjamin DeMott and I had planned the conference for the past two years, long before my article had appeared—postponed it— renewed our interest in it. Each of us would give position papers, there would be transcribed discussion, the proceedings would be published. Suddenly the meeting seemed terribly important to me, for through it I could take the issues raised by my article and place them in a national forum of education. . . . I wrote to the president: Would you join me in supporting this conference and have the college as a co-sponsor? No answer. . . . During those cold, dark days, when the attitude of the Central Administration remained intransigent, the conference seemed crucial to me. I felt asphyxiated by the college atmosphere—it had nothing to do with education. I had to escape this highly personalized, intensely politicized local fracas. . . .

I stopped responding to the media. Each media event simply perpetuated the superficial, gossip-laden aspects of the incident and inevitably led to distortion—to the need for further explanation. People remembered a story about a story about a story, and the argument of the article was forgotten. I waited for another campus crisis, but none came. The *Post* articles had faded into the record of scurrilous journalism: bad images of the college simply lingered in the minds of most people. A vice-president who had embezzled thousands of dollars from a consortium of urban colleges was in the news for a moment, but then gone—his was a singular, private aberration, and finally, it appeared, inconsequential.

No issue arose that was large enough to obscure me. And the letters back and forth in the campus newspapers simply kept the incident on everybody's mind. Each evening I would bring home some college communication— *The Campus* (a combination of news, reviews, and features), *The Observation Post* (a feature newspaper), *The Paper* (black news), *The Source* (Jewish news), *PM* (the evening session newspaper), and whatever fliers were generated from the whirring mimeograph machines. The number of communications on that campus seemed uncontrollable so that genuine communication was inevitably fragmented, the victim of limited financial support. All attempts at bringing out one solid, well-financed newspaper had collapsed before political pressures and you never knew when any single paper would appear. Communications everywhere but no communication.

I had thought that no response from me would help to end the matter—who can respond to silence?—but I had unleashed passions that were like flames switching across the driest brush on this campus. . . . Rumors reached me: The president was furious that he had lost important donations to his fund-raising campaign. The president was furious that he had to answer so many letters about this goddamned Gross affair. The president was furious at the alumni and some faculty who did not understand his larger vision and criticized him. The president was furious that no one appreciated all that he had done. . . . The president was furious. . . . He had sent his letter of self-defense and of public accusation, but that was no more than a public relations document; he had not yet spoken to me, and therefore had not settled the matter of my status. We both knew that. Through our silence, we realized that a meeting was inevitable—the only question was when and how the silence would be broken.

James Baldwin, who had been scheduled to appear before a college-wide audience, called from Paris to say he was looking forward to his appearance at The City College of New York. Together with a small group of black faculty—weeks before my essay had appeared—I had helped to plan the celebration of this occasion. In addition to all of the theatrical and musical events marking Baldwin's return to America after twenty years of exile in Europe, the author would be given the Martin Luther King medal. Everyone was gearing up for a major happening—the first news all semester, as someone said, that was positive.

James Baldwin. For me, the name carried a very special association—the name of an artist to whom I owed a private debt. This man had helped to shape my sensibility. In the 1950s he had opened my eyes to the world of Harlem—"Fifth Avenue, Uptown," "Notes of a Native Son," "The Harlem Ghetto"—and had created that city within a city for me as Hawthorne had Salem, Dickens, London, Dostoevsky, Leningrad—more real than the record of historians and sociologists, and far more memorable. I had written a tribute to him early in my career— "The World of James Baldwin"—and I had lectured on his work in Africa and Europe and Asia. "The Fire Next Time" was more than an essay to me: it was Jonathan Edwards in Harlem; it was exactly right in its passionate tension between the white and the black, between idealism and power, between the need for acceptance on the pragmatic level and the demand for a spiritual renaissance.

Most important, Baldwin was one of my teachers, more profound for not having been on the syllabus at Columbia University in the 1950s. So many ironies: before I had written my essay in *Saturday Review*, I had read and reread the beginning of "The Fire Next Time," holding the music of the language in my head, the intricate syntax, trying to capture it in my own description, especially in those first few sentences that had caused the greatest reaction. The style and passion of Baldwin's work had influenced me deeply, and I had wanted to inform an essay on education with the same sense of personal caring. So many articles about Open Admissions were blood-less, a battery of sociological statistics that no one read, whereas the experiment itself was as humanly passionate as any I had ever witnessed. But I had forced the scene too much, gone literary when I should have been more re-strained, drawn contrasts between the past and present and between "majorities" and "minorities" that were too dramatic and therefore open to misinterpretation. The subject was so sensitive, caring was not enough—caution was essential, too. Now, this man, James Baldwin, years after his expatriation, was coming home.

I went through his writing and excerpted passages for young black actors from our Performing Arts Center to read aloud. I wrote the president's remarks for him to deliver: "James Baldwin has had a lover's quarrel with America. . . ." And when Baldwin came to the college, the auditorium was filled and the president read my words and Baldwin delivered an impassioned speech that roused—as I later learned—the large audience.

I did not attend the affair. Its leader was from the black studies department, and though we had been personally cordial for the past eight years, we had also had ideolog-ical differences which had surfaced in my article as well as in his response to it, and I was in no mood for the pos-sibility of public flagellation. I had seen, in the 1960s, white liberals drawn and quartered for social inequities they could never have resolved, and I had seen too many cower before the epithets of militants who scarcely knew their names. I had no interest in being anyone's academic martyr.

Three weeks later, I received the first direct communication from the president in two months. The note stunned me.

April 6, 1978

Dean Theodore Gross
Humanities
The City College
Dear Ted,
Thank you for drafting my remarks for the James Baldwin ceremony on March 17.
I was delighted that the event was so well attended and went so smoothly.

Sincerely,

The letter arrived on Monday, April 11. A day later, the president's secretary called.

"The president would like to speak with you tomorrow," she told me on the phone. "At three? Are you free?"

Two months had passed. Not one word. Two months as all of these events had unfolded. Finally, the tension would be broken, and two people who had shared college problems long after the college day was done would now seek a solution to the one problem that is more important than any other, that lingers long after others have faded from memory—the personal problem, the human problem.

V

Through the president's reception room people come and go. The head of the union passes by. A month before, at a bustling faculty meeting, she had said to the president, "How can you work with a dean who disagrees with you?" Now she says, "Hi, Ted." No answer. "Not feeling too well today, Ted?"

I sit and watch the president's secretaries type and answer the telephone, as I have so often before. A year ago, when I was Vice-president for Institutional Advancement (a euphemism for fund-raising), these secretaries and I had crowded into my old Chevrolet to go to a cocktail party at a wealthy woman's home on Central Park South —to raise money for a chair in community medicine, named after the distinguished Harlem physician Arthur C. Logan, who had helped to establish our Center for Biomedicine. Bayard Rustin, Roger Wilkins, Ramsey Clark, Marion Logan, and others had been at the fund-raiser—and the secretaries and I had driven through Harlem like people with a purpose, a common purpose, down Central Park West, past the president's home, to the apartments along Central Park South, all of us working together to augment that dwindling tax-levy base of support, trying to figure a way to make The City College work. . . .

A public relations man walks by. . . . The Assistant Dean for Faculty Relations. . . . The black professor who had been chairman of the Department of Urban and Ethnic Studies before it was divided into separate departments of Black, Jewish, Puerto Rican, and Asian Studies. Student aides. . . . Figures in the corridors of a college that has been mine for an entire career.

. . . Suddenly I hear noises rising from within the president's office, as if the meeting is ending, then laughter, as the door swings open and a group—the Provost and Acting Dean of Community Relations, a professor of education—bursts out, passes me by.

The secretary buzzes the president.

"Dean Gross is waiting."

She turns to me and smiles—a half-smile.

"The president will see you now."

The office is huge. On one side it faces a nondescript, newly built science building and on the other St. Nicholas Park, rolling eastward into a Harlem that has not essentially changed for the twenty years I have come through its streets to The City College.

The president is positioned in the corner of his office, at an angle to me. In the eight years of his administration he has suffered a heart attack and stroke, but now he looks as though he has never been ill. He is standing near a metal coffee maker, holding a plastic cup in his hand, making a design in the cup of coffee with a plastic stirrer. Relaxed. Composed. Smiling.

"Coffee, Ted?"

"No, thanks."

He asks about the progress of a large grant proposal for which I have been responsible, "The Humanities, Preprofessional Education, and Public Policy," and which we will soon be submitting to the National Endowment for the Humanities. The success of this proposal has assumed enormous significance for a variety of reasons: tax-levy support is unreliable and there is no endowment to cover even cash-flow problems; enrollment has fallen off precipitously in liberal arts but has risen in the professional

schools; the majority of tenured faculty, middle-aged and
settled in conventional departments for the next fifteen
years before they retire, are teaching elective courses
with far too few students; the College of Liberal Arts and
Science has twenty-five departments, with hundreds of
offerings that often confuse the students; and—most importantly, most profoundly—no one has yet resolved the
tensions between career education and the humanities.
For all these reasons but primarily because the College of
Liberal Arts has lost its attraction for students, we are
developing this proposal. A heavy responsibility. The
need for its success has now taken on an air of despera-
tion, as if it can solve all of our problems. The proposal attempts to infuse career tracks with a humanistic perspective. It seeks to persuade young people, naturally driven
to careers, that literature and philosophy and history are
important. It asserts its central meaning in a capstone
seminar concerned with human values, which every student is required to take, linking public policy questions
with the practical world and the traditional study of humanities.[3] . . .

I describe some of the practical difficulties in encouraging faculty to work on this interdisciplinary proposal, and
we laugh at our common problems, administrators out
of their disciplines: the scientist, the humanist. "Sometimes," I report, "the chairmen of the so-called liberal arts
departments are as professionally minded as the most
hard-nosed dean of a professional school." . . . We are

[3] A full description of this proposal is given in Chapter 3, pp. 205–13.

loose, we are talking, we are pretending the past two months have not occurred. . . .

I sit in a chair. He settles on the couch, crosses and recrosses his legs. A coffee table separates us.

"We've been through quite a lot, Ted, you and I. I'm sorry I haven't answered your letters." My stomach turns sour. After the essay appeared, I had written him two letters—one private, apologizing to him and his wife for any hurt I might have caused them, and one that I reserved the right to make public but that, as things developed, I never did release. "I've been too busy answering so many other letters."

Then, finally, he talks—and the words rush out like a torrent.

"Why didn't you show it to me?"

"I knew you'd be angry."

We look at each other for what seems a very long time but is really only a moment—as though months of soul-searching have been squeezed into a fleeting glance. If I had shown him the essay (I am saying silently to him), it would have become an institutional document or it would not have been published at all. I knew he would be displeased with it, but I never thought he would personalize the piece so intensely, absorbing into himself aspects of Open Admissions that went clearly beyond any individual's control. The City College, *c'est moi.* . . .

"I could have helped you get it right," he said. "I could have prevented you from making errors." He rambled on about his current problems. "All the trouble I've had—now this." But after he talks through the agonizing difficulties of managing an urban college under the most adverse fiscal and political conditions, he brings himself up short, for he is a man of enormous pride, and remembers the purpose of the meeting.

"I understand you want to write a book on Open Admissions. . . . This essay is the first chapter? . . . All right, Ted. Take your sabbatical. Write your book. Come back in February 1979. We'll see where we are then."

The scientist as president speaks to the humanist as dean in a torrent of words that have been blocked up in his mind and shared only with administrators and friends and those who are forced to agree with him. Now he looks at me, through me, away from me, over me, smiling, smiling, smiling, trying to understand why I did what I did.

"You left out so much—the Biomed Center, the performing arts, legal studies—so much of what I've tried to do."

"I wasn't writing a public relations piece."

"I know, but it's a distortion. People think that this is all that happened."

"I don't pretend that this is all that happened."

"But everyone thinks so. They call me. They write me. All the alumni. Is this what has happened to City College? What am I to say? What would you say? They hesitate to give to the Development Campaign. They withdraw. What am I to say . . . ?" These questions must have drummed on for many minutes, and then, somewhere in the middle of the circular rhetoric, the real question finally emerges. "Why did you do this to me?"

"It's not about you, personally. As I said in my letter—"

"I'm sorry I didn't answer your letter. I've had so many to answer."

"It's not about you personally. It's about the institution. About you and me and other decent, intelligent people unable to shape the future of our institutions. You said it yourself two years ago. Remember how difficult it was to persuade anyone that the university should go from eighteen to thirteen colleges because we couldn't afford the size, because the number of students was diminishing? Remember the proposal to have underenrolled disciplines like classics put in one place, on one campus? Consolidation—some sort of consolidation? Every one of these attempts has been strangled by politics."

"Education is nothing if not political."

"I know. But you watch it and if you care and can't change anything fundamental, you write about it. At least I do. A humanist does. Maybe through analysis you'll effect change. Maybe. Ninety-two per cent tenure and the structure doesn't change. Paralysis. After a while it affects everyone in the system."

Round and round and then, like a leitmotif from the corner of his mind, the plan emerges:

"You want to write this book. Okay. Take your sabbatical. Come back in February. All right. We'll see where we are at that time."

The hours wear on. The words are repeated, the emotions laid bare. We are speaking to each other like friends and colleagues who have a future as well as a past. He tells me about a university and a city in which the budget, the people, the pressure groups—the enormous forces of modern bureaucratic education prevent a person from doing anything. Wear a man down. . . . He reminds me of how he almost left the college last year—his resignation had even appeared in the *Times*—until people prevailed upon him to finish what he had started—the urban educational model, foundering now because of fiscal crisis after fiscal crisis.

"But sometimes it's just too much. It takes an exercise of the will to overcome the pressure groups—and the never-ending budget cuts. It takes an exercise of the will to win this battle—an exercise of the will." I think of Ahab on the deck, of Don Quixote on his horse—and I remember this president charging into New York eight years ago, with a briefcase of brilliant and imaginative ideas, ready to convert a good college into a great university. . . .

His speech becomes discursive, and he smiles at me and expresses bewilderment at why I wrote the essay. Didn't I understand the larger plan, the deeper vision? Didn't I realize how the alumni would respond to this? How it would feed into their misgivings about Open Admissions? . . . But already I can sense the vision for him is growing less intense, less possible. Intelligence has come to calm that overweening will—the fire in his eyes is less brilliant—and he himself is looking past the college toward another future. . . . "You want to write this book?"

"I want to write it as well as I can. I'm not interested in name calling. That's the disease of this society. Radical, conservative, racist, anti-Semite, antifeminist. You label a

person and the problems vanish, they need no further
analysis—but the problems still fester. So far as I'm concerned, the deepest problem at City College—at every
place like City College—in the seventies is the language
problem. That's what the essay is essentially about. That's
the essence of Open Admissions, and we haven't begun to
solve it. I'm not sure we can solve it at the college level—
but I want to see the problem for what it is, not for what
it ought to be or might have been. I don't want to distort
the picture. I'd be glad to have your help, your criticism."

The broad benevolent smile.

"I'd like to read it. We'll make a devil's pact to go over
the manuscript together before it's published."

"I mean it."

"I mean it."

Finally: "Write the book. Take the sabbatical. We'll
see where we are in February." A handshake. A smile.
And I fix the words in my head as if they are engraved:
"Write the book. Take the sabbatical. We'll see where we
are in February."

VI

Two weeks later, I received the president's letter.

April 24, 1978

Dear [*sic*] Theodore L. Gross
Humanities
The City College
Dear Ted:
In accordance with our conversations, I shall recom-
mend to [the] Chancellor . . . and the Board of

Higher Education that you be granted a one-semester Fellowship Leave with full pay, for the period September 1, 1978, until January 31, 1979. Under recent BHE Policy, all cases of one-semester leaves, with pay, must be reviewed by the Chancellor. One condition of your leave is that you must return to the College for one year unless this condition is waived by the BHE.

During the period of your leave I trust you will not only be completing your book on Urban Education but will be preparing yourself to return to active teaching as a faculty member in the Department of English beginning February 1, 1979. I shall be appointing an Acting Dean of Humanities effective September 1, 1978, and expect that you will brief that person before your leave starts.

I wish to thank you for your years of service as Dean of Humanities at City College and to wish you success in your future undertakings.

Sincerely yours,

cc Chancellor ———
   Provost ———

I could not connect the letter with our conversation. Had he said anything that would lead to this letter? Had he even hinted at his decision? The repeated words that rushed to my head were, "Write the book. Take the sabbatical. We'll see where we are in February." And the tone had been one of reconciliation.

Certain thoughts must have coursed through his mind which he could not articulate, for whatever reasons; but I did not see why I should become his sympathetic interpreter. He was granting me a one-semester leave or sab-

batical at full pay—a rare privilege in the City University
at that time—and he was appointing an acting dean to replace me for the year, until a permanent dean was chosen. I felt as though I had been bought off. At the time,
my emotions were as raw as any wound, for I could not
believe what I read—and I could not believe that twenty
years of a career had become tinder on the altar of one
man's momentary fiery passion.

I lived with the letter on Wednesday, Thursday, Friday, and into Saturday and Sunday—and into those nights
and the mornings afterward. We talked about the options:

Take a year-long sabbatical (months before, I had been
offered a visiting professorship at a French university).

Appeal to the chancellor, to the Board of Higher Education.

Refuse to accept the conditions.

I could not leave for a year, for I knew this unresolved
controversy would haunt me in Paris. I could not appeal
the decision, for the president had obviously consulted
with the chancellor and the university's lawyers before
sending me this letter: the case was legally closed. I could
not refuse to accept the conditions of his letter. I was too
tired. Too tense. I was not born to be a martyr for academic freedom—or for any other principle. That was the
stuff of literature. . . . Twenty years ago—ten years ago—
one's image had been connected ideologically to this institution; one would have screamed about a violation of academic freedom or dissent because one would have cared—
really cared. Now, too many averted their eyes—taught

their classes—took their paychecks—found reality in their own writing or research or, if that too had died, in the next vacation—and treated the institution as though it were not a living thing where loyalty and affection were the measurable sentiments of a genuine career. Sad—to be so disconnected from one's work. Sad, to have to treat an institution—as only an institution. I knew that I could not accept this condition of existence, which I took to be the living death of a career. Thus, my essay. At the same time, I was not prepared to go to the stake for my freedom of expression: I was not inclined to draw swords with a president who had all the power. If necessary, I would quietly take my academic freedom elsewhere. It was, fortunately, a big country.

On Monday, May 1, I sent the president the note he wanted to receive:

> I have your letter of April 24, 1978, regarding the conditions of my one-semester Fellowship Leave with full pay, for the period September 1, 1978, until January 31, 1979.
> Consider this letter my written acceptance of those conditions.
>
> Sincerely,

On Wednesday, at the meeting of the Personnel and Budget Committee of the Humanities Division (so I was later told), the president advised the chairpersons from Art, Asian studies, Classics, English, Germanic and Slavic, Jewish studies, Music, Romance languages, Speech, and Theater Arts that a new acting dean would have to be appointed for a year.

"For the year?"

"For the year."

After this meeting (so I later learned), there was a news conference and a campus reporter asked the president about the Gross affair.

At three o'clock several chairpersons burst into my office.

"You didn't tell us. . . . When did he do it? . . . Why did he do it? I thought you said he had agreed. . . . Now? In May? He's mad. . . . For an article? . . . How can he do this? . . . It's an abridgment of academic freedom. It's intolerance of dissent. . . . This has to be the most politically stupid move. . . . You can't punish a man for what he wrote. Not at City College. Not in New York. Not in 1978. . . ."

But it had happened. And though my case was perhaps more dramatic than most, freedom of expression was in danger elsewhere, a subtle incursion that was the result of our conservative seventies. At The City College, the pattern seemed obvious. From the outset, Open Admissions had been so attacked by reactionary forces that the institution had become more and more addicted to public relations. Elsewhere, the fate of private colleges depended upon a positive image, too, and one listened to so many presidents champion institutions whose existence was questionable in the face of declining enrollments, diminishing populations—and the faculty in those institutions did not really speak, for fear of committing professional suicide. Thus, programs were often designed to attract students rather than offer the best education.

Officers of development and public relations and communications had become critically important in the modern university and would often be paid higher salaries than the most esteemed scholar. Faculties privately deplored this tendency, but were less critical publicly, for they knew the jobs of human beings were at stake. At The City College, the most vocal and vituperative opponent of Open Admissions on the faculty, the great public champion of standards who delivered speech after Ciceronian speech in the Senate forum and spoke of how the eloquence of the ages was being sacrificed to vocationalism and illiteracy suddenly grew far more tolerant when he realized that Open Admissions students were the majority of students at the college and provided a livelihood for the instructors he was addressing.

How can a college criticize a culture—one of its most intensely valuable functions—if it cannot criticize itself?

On Thursday morning, I was interviewed by a student reporter. On Friday morning the story of my forced resignation appeared in *The Campus*. On Friday afternoon a reporter from the New York *Times* reached me on the telephone: Was *The Campus* story accurate? Essentially, I said, then responded to her pointed questions very slowly, very cautiously, realizing the significance of this interview but never imagining the way it would be featured in the paper.

At eleven that night, the *Campus* reporter called.

"The story is in the *Times*."

"Where?"

"Page one. Do you want me to read it?"

"Where is it in the paper?"

"On page one. Do you want me to read it?"

I listened to him, but before I could collect my thoughts or respond, he snapped:

"You let him off the hook. All of you, always, let him off the hook."

I put down the phone, then heard it ring again. A reporter from the New York *Daily News*.

"Is that story true? . . . Boy, did you get a bum rap. Tell me what really happened."

I did—and my story was broadcast all next day on the radio station that the *Daily News* owned.

In Manhattan, at one-fifteen in the morning, I bought the New York *Times*.

CRITIC OF POLICIES AT CITY COLLEGE
ASKED TO RESIGN FROM DEANSHIP

A City College Dean who wrote a controversial article in which he criticized open admissions, "affirmative action," hiring policies, tenure and faculty unionism as "contributions to mediocrity" has been removed from his deanship, effective the end of this semester.

The dean, Theodore L. Gross, head of the division of humanities, said yesterday that the move followed "a mutual recognition on the part of the president and me that it would be wise for me to resign" in the wake of strong reaction on the campus to the article. The article appeared as the cover story in the February 4, 1978, issue of The Saturday Review under the title "How to Kill a Campus" [*sic*].

. . . Dean Gross, while acknowledging [the President's] right to assign or remove deans, said he believed the decision raised a basic issue of academic freedom of expression.

My weekend was a switchboard. Why did you say it was by mutual recognition? It wasn't. You should have blasted him. . . . How could he? Doesn't he realize this is contrary to the First Amendment? All you did was say the emperor has no clothes. . . . Horrendous for a university —it will create a chilling effect. . . . Radical groups have taken the law into their own hands. . . . He should have protected you and said: "I dislike what you've written but I'll defend your right . . ." . . . He's encouraged the Yahoos. . . . He doesn't want a critic so he fires him and reveals how intolerant of dissent he really is. . . . Your being fired reinforces the sense of a cover-up. A chilling effect. Indeed, the emperor has no clothes. . . . A threat to all of us in the classroom, in our writing, in our thinking—the abuse of power, administrative overkill. . . . You're being asked to pay the price for truth. . . . It's a hot issue—Open Admissions—you have to keep your mouth shut. You can't say anything at all; you certainly can't tell the truth. This kind of decision can have only one effect on a college campus—a chilling effect. . . . a chilling effect.

VII

On Monday morning, a small group of faculty had drafted a Statement of Principles:

INTELLECTUAL FREEDOM IN THE UNIVERSITY

A Statement of Principle

We are shocked, dismayed and outraged by the dismissal of Professor Theodore L. Gross as Dean of the Division of Humanities at The City College.

We are of different minds regarding the content of Dean Gross' article. Some of us feel it to be a telling description of the impact of Open Admissions on the college and university, others see it as partly or largely unreliable, distorted, misleading. Yet we are all agreed on a single point: that his right and the right of every member of the academic community to intellectual freedom must remain inviolate.

We recognize that deans of the college are appointed by the President and serve at his pleasure. We affirm the obligation of the President to remove a dean for incompetence. We understand the importance of agreement between the President and a dean on over-all college policy. However, we reject the notion that a dean should be removed because his perceptions do not match the President's on every significant issue, or because he publicly expresses divergent views.

We maintain that it is the obligation of a university to protect, even to cultivate the freedom to dissent. We maintain that any act that restricts freedom of expression strikes at the heart of what a university is charged to defend.

We therefore stand together in opposition to any overt or implicit restriction of freedom of expression, whether through harassment, or demonstration, or removal from office. We are appalled by the witch-hunting atmosphere which was fostered and abetted by some members of the central administration. We condemn all such attempts, and all those who support them through their words or their actions. We declare that the right to freedom of speech within an academic community is its most precious right and its profoundest cause. Let no one tamper with it.

(Signers will be listed alphabetically with departmental affiliation added for purposes of identification.)

The statement was signed by many faculty members, as it began to circulate throughout the campus. But the impetus of those who generated the petition was slowed by different reactions. Some chairpersons were fearful that their equipment budgets would be reduced if their names were known; some faculty had promotions or tenure pending and feared reprisals; others disagreed with my educational views; still others felt that a dean did not have academic freedom and served strictly at the pleasure of the president.

What undercut and ultimately emasculated the faculty petition were the politics of a modern university, expressed in terms of who controlled the budget and who made the real decisions. The greatest power is, after all, the power of persuasion, and faculties underestimate their own strength when they neglect it; but so many decisions in these years have been necessarily negative—firing faculty, reducing budgets—that most of the painful decisions have been left in the hands of a president. Once he makes those decisions he makes most of the others as well, and the transfer of power leaves the faculty largely reduced to its own rhetoric and, worse, to its own fear that the president will act arbitrarily. In this context, a principle, even of academic freedom, is considerably less momentous than one might think, given the realpolitik of a modern university. It remains a principle, easy to champion rhetorically but difficult to defend pragmatically, and the inevitable censures from national organizations like the American Association of University Professors or the ACLU carry little weight and are filed along with faculty petitions.

One morning a young faculty member stood before me, sweating.

"I've been up all night and I know I'm a coward, Ted, but I can't sign that petition. I have a leave coming up to France and I need it—need it. Okay, I'm a coward, but I'm afraid. I don't trust these people in charge. . . . It's like Russia. . . . Are we safe in this room?"

"Don't go on. I'm not your conscience."

The chairperson of the Faculty Senate sat in my office. Like me he had been at this college for twenty years. Two years before he had been fired as Dean of Students by this same president.

"Welcome to the club," he chuckled. But in a moment he grew serious. "We can't censure the president. Too much bad publicity. Who will replace him? We have to think of the college—for better or worse, he stands for the college. He'll be gone in a short time, anyway. . . . This could do great damage to the college, Ted, coming on top of the *Post* articles."

I did not argue. I felt that the Faculty Senate had become a forum largely perpetuated to receive information from the president and provost. It no longer concerned itself with action, nor did it challenge the authority of the president. Created in the late sixties, in response to the democratic impulse that raged through higher education, it had lost its power as budgets were slashed and crises often resolved quickly, arbitrarily, by the president and his staff.

Although there was outrage at the president's behavior and his bad timing, no one really challenged his authority. For many, the issue narrowed. Should an academic dean publicly criticize the policies of the institution in which he works? It was a vexing question, and I had considered it in its many ramifications. Scarcely anyone outside the president's cabinet would have objected to a dean's publishing an article, even one that called into question some of the practices at the university, in the *Harvard Educational Review*. No one would have objected to a dean's stating his own view in a public forum like a Faculty Senate, where student "stringers" for the *Times* and *News* were often present and did, on occasion, report the proceedings of critical events. Few would have been concerned at internal criticism gone public so long as the style had been appropriately academic.

It was, finally, a matter of personal style. The altered title was so dramatically offensive—the "private papers of a campus dean" implied revelations from the sanctuary—and the cover so vulgar, so intensely sensational, that it was hard to respond rationally to the article itself. One's mind was conditioned before reading the first word. And more important than any other consideration—so I like to believe—was that the essay had been written with passion, in a highly individualized style, for a magazine with national circulation, about deeply controversial issues upon which all who wish to survive speak euphemistically, with indirection, using qualifying phrase after qualifying phrase, in a kind of soporific language that mitigates meaning and purpose and certainly passion. Academic bureaucratize—the language of memoranda. I had written an essay that I thought was sensitive and perceptive, but it was taken personally by a president who attacked my character for my ideas—and it was taken personally by certain people because of a sentence here, a phrase there. Never had I known, so intimately, the power of the written word, its electric charge. Now that time had passed I regretted having used an indiscreet sentence here, an unnecessarily hard phrase there. By allowing only one aspect of a complex experience like Open Admissions to be published, I had been unfair to my own complex views. And it was particularly irritating that solutions had been omitted when I had spent these eight years engaged in nothing but attempting to solve the problems of Open Admissions.

But I had learned one thing—about myself, at least. If being a dean in an American college meant acquiescing totally to the power of a president; if one could not criticize past policies, as one worked loyally in the present; if one could not speak the truth for fear of losing one's job and lead rather than manage, formulate rather than follow; if one could not feel free to see one's own experience steadily and whole, then what was the point of being a dean in a university? Does a dean have academic freedom? The very formulation of that question, for me, is frightening.

For the first time, I realized the power of a front-page story in the New York *Times*. The media descended upon me as a hot news item. After receiving my approval to cover the story, a commentator from a local television station burst into my office with two cameramen, talking and snapping his fingers as he entered. "Here they protect this Marxist out west—what's his name, what the hell is his name?—and they dump on someone like you, who is trying to suggest some solutions to these agonizing problems. What the hell is happening to our colleges today?" He went on this way, almost shouting at me, interrupting himself, snapping his fingers as he tried to remember the Marxist out west, signaling to the cameramen that they should be preparing their equipment, using technical jargon. Then: "What was that guy's name out west? In Stanford, wasn't it? What's happening to our colleges? It's outrageous, so far as I'm concerned, outrageous. . . . What do *you* think? . . ."

And as I opened my mouth to utter my first words, he snapped his fingers again and the cameras flashed alive.

"What do you think, Dean Gross?"

For the moment, I could only think of T. S. Eliot: "I think we are in rat's alley/Where the dead men lost their bones." But I told the local television audience how dangerous I considered the suppression of opinion, how bureaucratized the university had become; and the com-

mentator (after he had interviewed the president, too)
ended his report: "Academic freedom? Well, that's the
question. It's all a matter of whose side you're on."

I was able to tell the same story to ABC and CBS and
Newsday and *Newsweek*—"The Scholar's Lament," ran
the story in *Newsweek*, with a picture of the students in
my office and a photo of me that resembled death. With
each report, waves of supportive letters flowed into my
office. The alumni, and educators generally, had been
highly critical of the president's action, and he was
champing at the bit. I learned that he was furious, raging
against the accusations that he had abridged academic
freedom and was intolerant of dissent. Privately he now
complained about my performance as dean, attributing
the declining enrollment in liberal arts to a failure of
leadership, telling people I should have done this, if I had
only done that—it was not *only* the article, it was more,
far more; but no one believed him, for I had been his favorite dean before the essay appeared, and they urged
him to refrain from going public with this criticism—"You
don't fire a dean, then dump on him." . . . And through it
all, I spoke to a class of graduate students about Dewey
and Faulkner and Ellison on Wednesday afternoons—and
sat at meeting after meeting shuffling papers without the
compensation of a future, sticking it out in the face of this
absurdity, as though one's personal performance would
make what was happening less absurd.

Someone from *Commentary* was writing a story about
the decline and fall of CUNY—would I agree to an extensive interview and be the star witness, the star victim, of

the piece? No, I answered: I refused to become Timon of the University. A highly regarded philosopher and social critic from the Center for Rational Alternatives was stunned at how I had been made a victim of academic freedom. He wanted to help. Would I answer questions? Would I write something for his newsletter? No, I said, but I would be happy to share with him the paper I had written on "Open Admissions and a Liberal Arts Education," soon to be delivered at the Rockefeller Foundation. That essay, after all, was my own rational alternative to some of the problems presented by Open Admissions.

VIII

On June 13, at nine-thirty in the morning, in the huge conference room of the Rockefeller Foundation, with coffee brewing in the corner and thirty participants in attendance, I did present my paper—the core of the final chapter of this book. Before I spoke, the foundation officers made their formal introductions and put the proceedings into a national context.

"Open Admissions was a very important educational experiment in dropping barriers, expanding horizons, widening opportunities for the poor. Society and institutions grow through continuity and through change, and in the late 1960s and early '70s, the time for change came once again—to the sons and daughters of new immigrants, and of different kinds of immigrants, some of whom may have even come in shackles to these shores—but the great questions were still the same: How much change, how much continuity? How do we widen opportunities and maintain standards of excellence, without which the very word education is meaningless? . . . . Open Admissions really represents a nation-wide problem—more than half the entering students at places like Berkeley and Wisconsin, not to speak of less selective colleges and of community colleges across the country, need some form of basic training in writing and reading. As citizens of this great city and of the larger society of which it is a part, we at the Rockefeller Foundation have witnessed this far-reaching experiment in education. We recognize its significance. We welcome the opportunity to analyze its record, its meaning for the future . . ."

Who was at the conference? Someone from FIPSE (the Fund for the Improvement of Post Secondary Education), someone from the Office of Education, the executive director of MLA (Modern Language Association), the director of Institutional Resources at CUNY, faculty from Amherst and Michigan State and Wayne, an officer from NCTE (the National Council of Teachers of English), the president-elect of Queens College, the chancellor of Long Island University, a large number of City College faculty —from Black Studies, the Urban Legal Studies program, the English department, the Political Science department —and, most visibly, the president of The City College. There had been private bets on whether he would come, but I had no need to bet—I knew he would be there, especially if I was there.

Two important exchanges occurred during that day.

One speaker called Open Admissions a flat failure. He

had been administratively involved in establishing the SEEK program in 1965, a program—the Search for Education, Elevation, and Knowledge—that gave stipends to underprivileged students with talent, and that was begun with the hope, as the speaker said, it would "self-destruct." "The fact that SEEK is bigger and better than ever is evidence of total failure. After thirteen, fourteen years, we still have not achieved the ability to teach the student reading, writing, and basic mathematical skills . . . which means now that college is not four, but five, six, seven, eight years, and a total failure." He was writing a book, the last chapter of which would be called "The Broken Promise": "The students essentially came to Open Admissions because they wanted to change their lives and what we have given them is the Broken Promise—there are not even jobs after they have our piece of paper." Thirteen years later, he asked: What have we learned of basic skills and the thinking process? Thirteen years later: What has been the social impact? Thirteen years later: Where are we? After all the vast expenditures and the expansion of the university and the endless experiments and the vast amount of human energy, where are we? In a politicized, bureaucratized university of a politicized city, without enough money to support its good intentions—and the dialogue hasn't changed. And what has been the good of it all? We have simply deceived those we promised and forfeited their hopes in the record of our failures. It has indeed been a Broken Promise.

"Well, there has been a considerable amount of good," Benjamin DeMott responded, with the perspective of someone outside the university. "For one thing, we have Professor Shaughnessy's book.[4] How many movements, essentially only a few years in intensity, have produced a document by a central figure in the drama—a book so definitive in its exploration of the problems? Furthermore, only a few years of formal experimentation have passed. You people have been the front-line people; you have burned the candles; it's only natural to be impatient and self-critical. When you say '66, '67, '68, '76, '77, you create an urgency in our minds, and as I hear you say those years, they stretch out and look like huge chasms, enormous tracts of time. But to anyone outside the situation and to anyone with what used to be called an historical perspective, six years, even thirteen years, does seem like

[4] DeMott's position paper, delivered in the afternoon, was a sensitive review of Professor Mina Shaughnessy's book *Errors and Expectations,* considered by many scholars and classroom teachers the most important book yet written on Open Admissions. DeMott's full essay—"Mina Shaughnessy: Meeting Challenges"—appears in *The Nation,* December 9, 1978, pp. 645–47.

Mina Shaughnessy had come into the English department of City College in the mid-sixties and, as Director of Basic Writing, had worked with me when I was chairman of the department, struggling with the impact of Open Admissions, training dozens of new young teachers who were torn between their Ph.D. work and their teaching of basic writing, always trying to make the system work, preserving thousands of student papers that ultimately served as the data upon which *Errors and Expectations* was based. For the past few years she had been Director of Institutional Resources for the entire university. In November 1978, she died, soon after she had received—as reported in *The New Yorker*—a "Presidential proclamation of International Literacy Day, 1978." In presenting the award for President Carter, Joseph Duffy, Chairman of the National Endowment for the Humanities, defined Mina Shaughnessy's career well: "Your work is a testimony to our concern not only for scholarship in humanities but for humanistic scholarship." As a human being and a leader of Open Admissions, she enhanced the quality of life in everyone—students, faculty, and administrators alike—who had the good fortune to know her.

a short time, indeed. It takes sometimes a long period to diagnose a social malady. . . ."

"We are really a remarkably impatient people," Mina Shaughnessy added, "especially about educational change. There was an attempt a while ago—do you remember it?—to develop some prototypes for a nuclear-powered aircraft. It took over ten years and millions of dollars. Not too many people were impatient about the fact that the prototypes were simply scrapped. The argument was that from that experience, there would be research, continuing research. On the other hand, we are attempting a revolution. I remember sitting once at a curriculum committee meeting, when everyone was feeling terribly gloomy, and saying something I still deeply believe: this is the most important college in the world because we are trying something that nobody has yet tried on such a scale. . . . It is ridiculous to talk about whether it will work or not work. The real need is to do the sort of research you would do if you were planning a nuclear-powered aircraft—we've never been given the funds for that research. The great questions, after you have the problem clearly stated, are, 'What is the next stage? What have we learned? What mistakes have we made? What do we do next?'"

DeMott agreed. "Yes. What is the next step—that's the question. Do we retrain teachers? Do we take this vision of what's gone wrong back into the school as it exists now in 1978? Or do we simply say that the miseducation of our children is a discipline problem and that the decline in scores is the consequence of poor discipline in the

schools? Too often, when people begin to talk about what
should happen in primary and secondary schools in an
urban situation, the talk goes very quickly away from
teaching and pedagogy and methods—that personal encounter back and forth between teacher and student—to
externals like how many policemen must be in the halls to
prevent teachers from being murdered. . . . We now
have this very useful piece of work—*Errors and Expectations*—about why those scores have gone down and will
keep on going down. We have an 'Anatomy' of the Open
Admissions experience. Now, to use the cliché, we stand
at a crossroads: What is the next step?"

The second exchange was equally important.

The president, who had identified himself all day as a
scientist among humanists, turned to DeMott and asked a
simple but fundamental question: "As a person in humanities, do you see how we can take this understanding
of particular writing experiences and situations and
make the connection with a liberal arts education? How is
the connection finally to be made between Open Admissions and a liberal arts education?"

DeMott hesitated before he answered: he had finished
his paper, he said, "And we have to bear in mind, Mr.
President, how much enthusiasm there is for one person
who's just given one paper to start giving another." But
he could not resist the opportunity to begin an answer. . . . "The impact of Open Admissions upon liberal
arts—the democratization of educational opportunity in
this society—will change the character of liberal arts. It
will change people's understanding, the way in which

they put forward the tradition. It is not enough to say we will modify the tradition by having world literature instead of Western literature or add ethnic studies and area studies or say that we will acknowledge continents other than this one—these are inevitable developments. When the spokesmen for the liberal arts adequately perceive their social and political situation as citizens of a democracy, the nature of those disciplines won't change, but their content and method will—you can feel the ice already breaking. The relationship between Open Admissions and liberal arts is like the relationship between embryonic democracy and democracy itself."

The statement was a first step—tentative, exploratory—suggesting how education needs to be organically rooted to its learners and its society, without any necessary sacrifice of standards. Perhaps the texts will change: *Let Us Now Praise Famous Men* instead of *Silas Marner*. Perhaps the methodology will include more activity on the part of students. Perhaps, if we are honest and look at the central question of what sort of coherent liberal arts education can be offered to the majority of our students today, we too must be tentative, a little humble before the huge changes that have beset us within these twenty years: student revolutions, Open Admissions, technology, mass communications, a shrinking job market. "In a city"—to use Saul Bellow's language. "In a century. In transition. In a mass. Transformed by science. Under organized power. Subject to tremendous controls. In a condition caused by mechanization. After the failure of radical hopes. In a society that [is] no community and devalue[s] the person. Owing to the multiplied power of numbers which [have] made the self negligible."

A new synthesis for the humanities must emerge from the concatenation of new learners, who justifiably demand entrance to our universities, and our traditional insistence upon standards. We haven't the right to deny standards to these new learners and we have the obligation, in a democratic society, to include them in our universities.

When we regard the educational record of earlier schooling during the past twenty-five years, we begin to see how critical the success of Open Admissions will be in the future—for all levels of learning—and how central the humanities must be to that future. It seems clear that efforts at integration in the lower schools have, for the most part, failed; it also appears that community control, although an important element in decentralization, has resisted integration. Each attempt at integration results in further bureaucratization and centralization of the system —someone has to order it to happen—while community control often usurps the authority and self-determination of teachers themselves. As a consequence, schools seem managed at a greater and greater distance from the children who need them and poor people remain segregated in their poverty. As Michael Katz has pointed out, schools are still distant and alien institutions to the poor. Teachers do not run the schools and are harassed by administrators. American education remains "universal, tax-supported, free, compulsory, bureaucratic, racist, and class-biased."

Given the vast bureaucracy of public education in every city of this country, realistic and honest solutions that go beyond conservative or radical rhetoric are extremely difficult to implement. Politicians may blame educators every time poor reading scores appear, and reformers may claim that the current system is unworkable. The party of reaction may cry for law and order as the ultimate solution and the party of reform may call for alternate modes of education—but if we have learned anything from these years, we know that the bureaucracy is ours for the foreseeable future, that large social ills cannot be reformed by education alone, and that there are no utopias to solve the broad, complex problems of democratic education in our complex democracy.

I leave law and order and punitive modes of demanding standards to others—these negative approaches are too self-limiting, too absolute, in a society where whole groups of immigrants and minorities have suffered historically from their implicit exclusiveness. I leave to still others the recommendations for income redistribution and for reform measures that would exert external social or political pressures upon schools—they are often attractive but too generalized for someone who has not seen them effected during the half-century of his life. For the moment, we have these difficult problems confronting educators in an urban educational system that has not changed for more than one hundred years and that will not, so far as I can see, fundamentally change. The moment has already been more than a moment far too long. However bureaucratized the school system may be and however difficult it is to implement integration and sensible community involvement within that system, it is the structure that we have and that we must make flexible by reaching through it, as directly as possible, toward the school children themselves. A real hope for integration, community involvement, and decentralization of authority—essential goals in democratic education—can be first developed at the college level, through a new synthesis for the humanities that informs the meaning of Open Admissions and that will set directions for earlier levels of education.

This new synthesis must be formulated by humanists who possess an open-mindedness and flexibility and respect for diversity; who believe that the development of basic skills and a liberal education are not two separate activities; who know that adult learners without appropriate skills are not hopelessly flawed; who are not yet willing to be only academic servants for everyone obsessed by pre-professional education; who assert the value of the person as essential—especially in a democracy. As one humanist who has known the social crosswinds plaguing liberal arts, who was trained intellectually to cherish a culture born of history as he has struggled pragmatically for a future in which that culture could continue to be meaningful, I offer one kind of synthesis in my final chapter—an elaboration of the paper I presented at the Rockefeller Foundation, modified by those who sat at the larger conference table on that day in June, and chastened by these events that I have described.

IX

My academic drama ended with the end of classes. One day, the students were gone and the campus desolate. Administrators met and worried about the budget presentation to state officials, about falling enrollments, about the future of the College of Liberal Arts and Science, about candidates for tenure in a college that was already 92 per cent tenured. A reporter from the New York *Times* had been on campus, preparing a major story about The City College. When it appeared on June 19 and 20, the general reaction was that it was favorable. But the president was dissatisfied—not favorable enough. Someone on his staff had said the college was "inflexible," and he was angry. The brief editorial on the following Saturday, June 24, was, however, unqualifiedly positive and seemed to answer the title that the *Saturday Review* had imposed upon me. Those *Saturday Review* editors had hurt me— who knows how much?—by calling my essay, "How to Kill a College: The Private Papers of a Campus Dean." The title of the New York *Times* piece read: "City College Lives." And the editorial that followed could have been written by our public relations office.

The City College does indeed live, and it has surely passed through a painful period of adjustment. Its entire history has been an adjustment to the poor people of New York: 133 years of New York City and America breathe in the cracks and corners of its buildings. One remembers the passionate passages of *David Levinsky* as the hero regards the faces of all those future civil servants even more than the Nobel Prize winners and other celebrated Americans—the Irish, Italian, Jewish, Hispanic, oriental, black people who have worked their way into the middle class, who have traveled up from poverty, Horatio Algers running to succeed. Hungry. Abrasive. Frightened. Motivated. Speaking with foreign accents. Arguing. Dissenting. Learning the discourse of success. Strange avatars, these children of immigrants, of a democratic mythology. More perhaps than any other institution, The City College of New York has tendered this remarkable mythology to the American poor.

And because of its democratic character as a nation of nations, The City College has boasted the greatest tradition of dissent and academic freedom. These principles were its power, its glory: it dared to disturb. For a moment that tradition was broken in me. But the meaning of this particular event goes far beyond the personal struggle between a president and his dean. It goes to the very purpose of a university, devoted to concepts that are in danger of becoming no more than clichés: academic freedom, tolerance of dissent, independence of mind. For a university is not an army or a business or a public relations firm—no general or accountant or huckster can be allowed to steal away its independence. When there is internal intimidation and suppression of an individual's thought, then the chilling effect occurs, and everyone becomes circumspect, and the external forces—the legislature and private donors who support us, the many political pressure groups that view the university in terms of their own narrow interests—may begin to dictate academic policy. Our strength is in our independence as responsible educators. The thought is simple and yet profoundly important. There will be no future for the humanities if we cannot determine it, and the recommendations anyone may have—however revised by us as educators—will be lost to some form of expediency.

The City College has already absorbed the experience that I have described, and, one hopes, it will prosper. The years ahead will be lean, as they will be for most colleges across this country: contraction in faculty, decline in enrollment, the continued need of students for training in basic skills, budget restraints that discourage experimentation and research and travel. Public colleges, dependent on tax-levy dollars, may be held so visibly and narrowly accountable in their performance—"how many hours is that teacher actually in the classroom?"—that they will stand in danger of losing those features that should make them the intellectual leaders of a society: time to think about the problems besetting education and, by extension, of American culture; time to do the research that will make sensible experimentation possible; time to ask the right questions of social and political institutions and make recommendations for solutions.

The myth for most of us must be that of Sisyphus—Camus's Sisyphus—we must learn to relish the quest. The needs are clear: a more coherent curriculum; stronger articulation with high schools; a sensible relationship between the humanities and pre-professional education; lifelong learning that extends the meaning of the university; the humanization of our culture through ourselves as humanists. These recommendations inform my final chapter.

For twenty years I traveled to work at The City College of New York. Too many of the people in its Harlem neighborhood are now mired in poverty as they were in 1958. Still, there is an office building on 125th Street that was not there, co-operative apartments on Lenox Avenue, a new theater on The City College campus. For twenty years, I witnessed the middle class leave the city to the wealthy and the poor. Still, The City College now has something like 33 per cent black students, 22 per cent Hispanic, 7 per cent oriental, and the balance composed of various ethnic whites. It is now and will continue to be, as a consequence of Open Admissions, a more faithful microcosm of New York and urban America and the world, building a new middle class. Progress? Perhaps. Too slow? Certainly.

One realizes the complex urban conditions that make progress so agonizingly slow as one fights for a future. The sixties taught us the limitations and possibilities of the university. It cannot solve social problems rooted outside itself, but it can identify those problems, alter social and moral behavior, and even cause a war to terminate—the power of the academic conscience can be very powerful indeed. Open Admissions taught us that only through careful planning and a sensible educational design can we hope to approach success, to know the limitations our success might have, to be a little humble before the overwhelming task we assume; but it also taught us one of the greatest lessons of these past twenty years. By opening our academic doors, we can touch the minds of people never seen before in a college classroom and thus prepare for the reformation of our society. The promise of Open Admissions is very powerful indeed. One may have to accept the physical constraints of academic life, but one need never surrender its promise for more and more students as one works one's way up the various streets that lead to The City College—to the city colleges of America —where the future of this country will be determined.

Is there a meaningful future for the humanities at these urban institutions? We can only answer yes, for our colleges will no longer serve their fundamental function as a conscience for the nation if we fail to forge a humanistic future for them. We need to give students all the knowledge we possess and all the skills they need, but we must educate their conscience and imagination as well. Is there any more important purpose to a human being's career? To a student's education?

THREE

A Future for the Humanities

What have I learned from the experience of Open Admissions? And what future for the humanities can I recommend from these experiences?

Can Open Admissions and academic excellence coexist, given the imperatives of a college education? Is this 133-year-old experiment, as defined by the first president of The City College, still worth pursuing: "the experiment is to be tried, whether the highest education can be given to the masses, whether the children of the people—the children of the whole people—can be educated and whether an institution of learning of the highest grade can be successfully controlled by the popular will, not by the privileged few"?

Surely this educational experiment has become the dominant form of learning in this country—from California to Texas, from Wisconsin to Pennsylvania. In one form or other the tension—the apparent contradiction—between total access to our colleges and the selective admission of students who can carry on the sophisticated work of higher education troubles all of us—especially those who draw their funds from the public sector. One wants the jewel in the crown of a state system—Binghamton and Albany, Austin, Madison, Berkeley, University Park—but one needs the community colleges for those who have not yet excelled or whose excellence may be more pragmatically oriented, who may need a campus that is smaller and nearer to home and less immediately demanding.

For in the perspective of history this experiment at The City College of New York and at all of the land-grant institutions throughout the nation has been primarily a success. We cannot afford to sacrifice the many variations on a democratic theme without surrendering part of ourselves as Americans: a need to be just to those who have been excluded from the richness of our culture; a willingness to offer a second chance to those who failed at an early age; a constant reassessment of the students' interests and goals at every stage of their academic careers. Deep in our roots are Jefferson and Emerson and Douglass and Lincoln and Whitman and Ellison—idealism as well as pragmatism, becoming more than being, openness rather than exclusion, a future that repudiates prejudices of the past. We are a generous people—whatever evils have often contradicted our collective, idealistic character—and Open Admissions, with all of its problems and even its waste, is a natural result of democratic education, an expression of that "popular will" first articulated more than a century ago.

At the same time, we are an intensely competitive people, and we naturally want our children to have strong training in basic skills, small classes, internships, tutorials, special programs, the most brilliant faculty we can afford —in a word, excellence. We want them to be educated in colleges "of the highest grade" even as we want those colleges "successfully controlled by the popular will."

Since the Second World War the demands placed upon our colleges—and upon social institutions generally—have changed dramatically and irrevocably. Consider, for example, the impact of soldiers returning from several wars and being offered open access to our colleges. Like the current Open Admissions students, these veterans have often been first-generation college students, highly motivated and often academically unprepared; their effect, most intensely realized after the Second World War, has been liberating for universities and has provided the first intimation of today's most powerful phenomenon in higher education—adults returning for post-professional training or continuing education. The benefits accorded veterans as well as the financial aid for a later generation of the underprivileged—in the form of SEEK and other subsidized programs—have contributed to the rising expectations and opportunities of people who at one time in our history would never have contemplated schooling beyond the secondary level.

Consider, from another point of view, an economy that has changed from manufacturing to service and that is driven by a technology so automated those who once were content with manual training now seek jobs demanding the skills of higher learning. Then the impact of television has been pervasive and profound. It is still difficult to measure its full impact, but surely television has made the written word seem less significant to youngsters and has contributed to the decline in reading scores at the same time as it has nourished the expectations of poor people to riches they never would have seen or known before. Demographic changes have simply aggravated the problems for urban schools, as truancy and other manifestations of a disaffected population have made training in basic skills difficult to achieve.

All of these social forces in the past thirty years have converged to create the inevitable demand for Open Admissions on the part of minorities. Certain industries, like construction, may have been temporarily able to exclude the underprivileged from their ranks in an ugly form of racism; but education fortunately has had no choice, and because it has been essentially the only major social institution committed to Open Admissions it has been the most vulnerable—the most criticized. For the first time in our history, the many different constituents of our culture have come together on a campus and forced us to consider the full implications of democratic education.

How can we yoke together these two aspects of America—the individual and the masses, the private person's need for self-expression and excellence and the group's demand for accommodation, for access? How can we marry classicism—the culture of the ages—with the social purposes of the underprivileged, the academically unprepared? How can we unite, to borrow the words of

Van Wyck Brooks, the "highbrow" and the "lowbrow," the theoretical and the practical, the "cultivated public" and the "business public," in one educational enterprise— a distinctively American enterprise that is neither solely committed to liberal arts nor exclusively grounded in professional training? How can we realize Dewey's critical description of "the democratic ideal":

> A democracy is more than a form of government; it is primarily a mode of associated living, of conjoint communicated experience. The extension in space of the number of individuals who participate in an interest so that each has to refer his own action to that of others, and to consider the action of others to give point and direction to his own, is equivalent to the breaking down of those barriers of class, race, and national territory which kept men from perceiving the full import of their activity. These more numerous and more varied points of contact denote a greater diversity of stimuli to which an individual has to respond; they consequently put a premium on variation in his action. They secure a liberation of powers which remain suppressed as long as the incitations to actions are partial, as they must be in a group which in its exclusiveness shuts out many interests.

How can we, accepting this formulation as fundamental to American education and life, translate the ideal characteristics of democracy into a successful union between Open Admissions and academic excellence?

These are hard questions that deserve straight answers. For we may lament the decline of literacy or the end of education or the crises in the classroom or the inadequacy of our current school system, but we know that the language problems of Open Admissions represent the reality of American schools and that a liberal education must grow organically from that reality. Only through solutions to the problems posed by Open Admissions will we have a future for the humanities. And those solutions, though rising from the democratic conception in education and its theoretical truths, must be as pragmatic and plain as a daily lesson plan one knows can work. The time for lamentation is over: a new synthesis for the humanities is needed.

I

The first lesson I learned from Open Admissions was that we need to retrain teachers, from first grade throughout college, in the instruction of writing and reading, of composition and literature. When I was chairman of the English department, at the outset of Open Admissions, my colleagues and I organized a conference, "Our Mutual Estate," that brought together the chairpersons of English in the New York City high schools and the faculties from English departments throughout the City University.[1] As a group, they addressed themselves to a range of

[1] In this chapter, I will be referring to programs and plans that have been developed during the past ten years. Each of them has required the co-operation of many friends and colleagues in the educational community of New York City and throughout the nation. It would be distracting to name my associates above; but they must be named, for everyone knows that in reality an idea is only as good as those who implement it. Thus, this chapter will become a kind of *passacaglia* of my administrative career: in the treble, the ideas; in the bass, the people

problems in language and literature that affected junior and senior high school teachers as well as college instructors: creative writing and composition; mass communications and the study of literature; a sequential study of writing and literature. These educators, who have met annually since then, are most conscientious and pragmatic. Many of the secondary school instructors were City College students before Open Admissions was implemented—indeed, we in the English department, and in the liberal arts college generally, were not sufficiently sensitive to the fact that, years ago, we were teaching future teachers of the New York City school system. Like so many professors of English throughout American colleges, we left pedagogy to the School of Education, in a kind of academic *noblesse oblige,* and we missed extraordinary opportunities to bridge theory and practice, to help lay a foundation for the future study of the humanities.

The confusion in the humanities stems largely from this self-absorption in our research-oriented "disciplines," which explore the theory of language acquisition and literary criticism, in the separated practical application of foreign languages and speech—in an isolation from other

who humanized the ideas. It seems to me important, moreover, in my desire to be as authentic as possible, to describe my own reality in New York—to establish, as Thoreau once said, my own *point d'appui*—and then to make references to other programs elsewhere in the nation.

"Our Mutual Estate" would have been impossible without the cooperation of Anita Dore, Director of English at the New York City Board of Education, and her colleagues in the secondary schools. It would never have been mounted with so much success without the sensitive supervision of Norman Levine, Professor of English at The City College of New York.

forms of culture that has led to an internal, structural atomization of general education. We have paid a dear price for having grafted a graduate school sensibility on to the undergraduate education of future teachers, for having distinguished skills from "substance," pedagogy from research. Speech is now a discipline separate from English; reading is taught in a School of Education or in remedial programs. By reasserting the interdisciplinary character of language and literature, especially through the retraining of teachers, greater coherence will inform the humanities so that developed skills and breadth of knowledge will be organically linked.

The secondary school administrators who participated in "Our Mutual Estate" had been tested and had survived in the crucible of urban education where theory is often lost to the overwhelming necessities of the practical. They knew the importance of Open Admissions and accepted its responsibilities, and were willing to participate in the retraining of teachers in their own schools. Their numbers can be replicated throughout the cities of America.

Articulation among teachers from first grade through college is essential. Together, school and college instructors must develop a sequential study of writing from first grade through the second year of college so that everyone's expectations in the educational continuum are clear. The finest classroom teachers—assistant principals or chairpersons wherever possible, but always the exciting and excellent instructors for whom teaching is an art as well as a craft—should be provided with partial fellowships that allow them to participate in college workshops where curriculum materials, teaching strategies, and the latest research on language acquisition are discussed. These "master teachers" should subsequently lead workshops in their own schools, sharing with their colleagues all that they have learned and the curriculum materials they have acquired in the college workshops. It is important that the teachers remain actively involved in their home schools while they have their fellowships so that there is a reciprocal relationship between their everyday tasks and the workshops that allow them to reflect upon their profession.

The specific implementation of this plan is relatively simple. One-year teacher-fellowship programs should be developed in clusters of fifteen instructors, preferably within the same school district: twelve teachers (one in each grade, from one through twelve), two college co-ordinators (one from the writing staff and one from the reading staff, responsible for supervising the development of the fourteen-year sequential writing curriculum), and one evaluator.

The programs should move in three stages, beginning with a pre-workshop spring seminar in which the teachers will *study* the research in writing and reading; *write* in order to understand the problems students confront when given assignments;[2] *create* with other members of the

[2] Teachers writing to improve their own skills as well as to appreciate the difficulties of their students is a fundamental element in one of the most successful writing projects yet developed—the Bay Writing program at the School of Education, the University of California at Berkeley.

The language problems of school children are directly related to the fact that many teachers are not as fluent as they might be. Michael Crosby, Director of Admissions for Fordham University, has pointed out

cluster appropriate teaching materials for the various grade levels; *evaluate* the effectiveness of the developed materials in their home classes; *consider* solutions to the great problem in writing instruction: the teacher's need to correct as many as 175 essays a week.

The second stage involves a summer writing workshop during which each instructor in the fellowship program teaches one writing workshop that serves as a laboratory for testing the materials developed during the pre-workshop seminar; I will amplify upon the summer workshop shortly.

The third stage is a post-workshop seminar. Having tested their curriculum materials in the summer workshops, the teachers will now refine them, prepare them for publication and for distribution in their schools, and make plans to conduct in-service teacher training programs of their own, one of the conditions of the fellowship. Throughout the fellowship program the evaluator, who should be drawn from outside the school district and the college, will test the effectiveness of the teaching materials as they are created during the year.

As soon as one broaches an idea like a teacher-fellowship program or (as I will soon suggest) tutorial support and the publication of a sequential curriculum in writing and literature, the first legitimate question—

---

that despite our lamentation about the pejorative influence of television on the verbal skills of children, the quality of English spoken on the medium is superior to that which is usually heard in the average classroom.

especially in an age of the taxpayer revolt—is, "At what cost? What is the bottom line?" Certainly, however one measures the educational results of Open Admissions, everyone who participated in it would agree that the city and state were not prepared to finance the experiment—in this sense, Open Admissions was a broken promise. Hiring twenty-one full-time faculty members in the summer before Open Admissions began, as I did in 1970, and then being forced to fire them year after year because of constant budget cuts is no prescription for educational planning, faculty stability, or academic success; yet this was the shifting, ever-growing shadow cast upon us—and, of course, it hovers still, as the student population diminishes inexorably and administrators wait for faculty to retire or resign. Thus, when I speak of programs I instinctively consider cost, the lowest possible cost, like any administrator who has survived the seventies. And as someone who worked toward the creation of a public/private university, I believe its meaning is particularly justified in these fundamental proposals I am presenting.

The year-long teacher-fellowship program is a modest proposal indeed: $3,500 for each partial fellowship (and this includes work in a seven-week summer session); $4.00 an hour or course credit for tutors who aid each teacher; and a small amount—$2,000—for supplies. The total request for fifteen fellows on year-long appointments—i.e., one "cluster"—is $67,500—a small sum, it would seem, when one estimates the number of other teachers and students (350 in a summer writing workshop alone) each fellow affects in his development of curricular materials and in further teacher-training seminars.[3]

Yet, when I took this proposal to the thirty-fifth floor of a city bank in New York, where a group of vice-presidents listened patiently, and showed the film of a summer pilot project that demonstrated the possibilities of the proposal and the subsequent progress of these students—extraordinary progress in a very short period of time; when I spread before the vice-presidents testimonials from key educators at the New York City Board of Education; when I tried to persuade them that the city bank was also responsible for the education of New Yorkers who might one day work in or use their bank, the vice-presidents showed me fear in a handful of congratulations.

Their reason for rejection was simple: "We believe in your program, Dr. Gross. . . . We believe that you have attracted superb teachers and trained college tutors. We know that your colleagues include some of the principal experts in language training and that you've learned a great deal through Open Admissions. . . . We agree with you that one really effective way of solving this problem is through teacher training and a cadre of conscientious tutors. . . . We even accept your contention that the city bank has a responsibility to help a college, publicly supported, in solving these problems. It *is* our common city and we do have to pool our common resources. But—but— however effective you and your colleagues may be, we do not believe your program can be institutionalized in the New York City school system—and that is our deepest

[3] The details of the program budget are in Appendix 1.

concern. You have a model—an excellent model that will undoubtedly work well—but can it be institutionalized? We do not believe so. The Board of Education has a budget of more than $2 billion and it has not even begun to solve the problem. Why should we assume that our meager contribution of $67,000 will make any difference? Good luck, Dr. Gross. God bless you, Dr. Gross. Yours is a worthy cause."

Cordial, civilized, and deeply depressing. . . .

As I descended the elevator shaft, I thought of the refrain in *Slaughterhouse Five* that follows each slaughter: "So it goes . . . so it goes." But my first reaction of disappointment in the conservative response of the city bank executives was really typical of someone who had been protected by the academic world, someone who had spent his career teaching "Bartleby the Scrivener" and *The Gilded Age* and *The Financier* and *Death of a Salesman* and dozens of other texts in which he had seen business as the enemy of the sensitive soul, and criticized it accordingly. I had been a member—to use Van Wyck Brooks's imagery again—of the "cultivated public" and had scorned the "business public," but now that I wanted to engage the support of businessmen (most of whom were quite cultivated), the neat divisions were not so neat any longer. At least, I had to reconsider my position.

The vice-presidents of this city bank were, from their perspective, understandably cautious. We cannot even persuade our city, state, and federal legislators to support new programs in the area of literacy. We find ourselves controlled by a budget that scarcely allows for operating expenses. We seem always in a defensive posture as we claim the need for remediation and spend so much time protecting ourselves from a shrinking budget. We do not seem to be a good investment. As disappointing as my experience was, I now realize that the vice-presidents reacted like responsible leaders of any private corporation or foundation; they looked for evidence of some institutional support before taking a risk themselves. Although we had supported three summer programs through tax-levy dollars and had provided college facilities, our gesture was minimal—we had taken no real risk ourselves. We did finally receive token outside support from J. Walter Thompson, the New York *Times*, and the New York *Daily News* that allowed us to continue these projects, but we could not do enough, and the experience was particularly frustrating.

The dimensions of this frustration are instructive, I believe, for they involve the concrete difficulties of failing to move forward in one large public system of education, despite the good will of so many administrators and teachers, despite the attempt of many sympathetic educators to create what I still feel is essential—a National Center for Literacy. Let me be personal.

In the course of seeking support for these proposals that centered upon improving the language skills of school children, I had the good fortune of meeting and collaborating with a vice-president of J. Walter Thompson, who, with the support of the advertising agency, was deeply interested—personally and professionally—in solving the problems of illiteracy. The two of us, in our attempt to establish a National Center for Literacy, moved on two tracks that were ultimately to meet. My colleagues and I developed the teacher-fellowship proposal, and I made presentations before groups of high school principals and superintendents in the Bronx and Manhattan, before key executives at the Board of Education and the state education department, and received their collective endorsements. At the same time, the vice-president of J. Walter Thompson met with different groups—executives of newspaper chains, magazines, pharmaceutical companies, food corporations. Whenever I joined these meetings I was amazed at how many different groups in the American economy depend upon literacy for their survival, how much self-interest informs the business community in terms of needing to improve the level of literacy, how inextricably fused the public and private sectors are, how much we need each other. And, apart from whatever social conscience the leaders of an ad agency may have (far more, I have discovered, than most academicians would allow), advertisers need print as well as television to sell products: it is far cheaper, in many ways, and more effective.

But as attracted as many of these corporate executives were to our idea of a National Center for Literacy—one that included a research unit, a publications unit, a unit devoted to practical programs—their resistance always resembled that of the vice-presidents from the city bank. They worried about our ability to institutionalize the plan, and they wanted some one institution—a college, a school system—to support it, with tax-levy dollars. But every time I returned to my own institution, there were no dollars—there was barely enough money to keep the current remedial programs afloat. Thus, my frustration at the time—but not, I must say, any loss of belief in the validity of these proposals. On the contrary. . . .

Two years have passed. . . . In retrospect, the problem was certainly New York City—its enormity, its high degree of bureaucratization, its suffering from one of the most severe fiscal crises in its history and its consequent refusal to accept the financial burden of the City University, its transfer of responsibility to the state so that any new idea, however compelling, seemed quixotic in an atmosphere of Armageddon. The plans need a more modest compass for their success, a smaller city, a reasonably stable tax-levy support that corporations and foundations can trust.

In any event, the view of the corporate executives must be altered by economically defensible proposals whose results are measurable—proposals that will help cure the paralysis that has gripped public education and that will, initially, enjoy the support of a single institution, then the city and the state so as to engage in turn support from the private sector. The responsibility is ours—the financial support in that private sector is there.[4]

[4] In addition to individual corporations, many of which have foundations for this purpose, an organization through which financing can be solicited is the Economic Development Council in New York.

The American Association of Advertising Agencies has become specifically concerned with the problems that attend illiteracy. It has sponsored a document, "Reducing Functional Illiteracy: A National Guide to Facilities and Services," which lists by city, county, and state the organizations throughout the country that are committed to reducing il-

At the same time, it is important to stress that industry has an obligation to set more than minimal guidelines for employment. There have been many attempts to improve the language skills of employees once they are on the job —A.T.&T., Chase Manhattan Bank, New York Insurance, and other companies have in-training programs; but industry has not really indicated in any comprehensive or direct manner the competencies essential for initial employment. Once industrial leaders demand certain levels of literacy and learning, students will make a fuller and more direct connection between their education and the world of work.

II

A sequential curriculum in writing, which naturally develops from the teacher-fellowship program, constitutes the second lesson that I learned from Open Admissions, one that has become especially significant as I have worked with elementary, junior, and senior high school teachers. There is a need for a national curriculum in writing skills, and a committee of the most significant educators in the field of composition, sponsored by an organization like the National Council of Teachers of English, the National Endowment for the Humanities, the Modern Language Association, or a private foundation,

---

literacy. The document is published by Contact, an organization led by Gary Hill in Lincoln, Nebraska. The 4 A's, working through "Contact Center," will attempt to support local facilities throughout the nation by financing specific programs or by identifying sources of financial support.

should be assembled to design one and publish it for the use of educators everywhere in this country. Although I have some views about the college-level curriculum, I would not pretend even to recommend what the sequential study of writing should be—this is a committee effort, and not only of English educators but of psychologists and librarians and counselors as well.

My suggestion is not in support of a mindless "back-to-basics" movement, a "lock-step instruction in prose mechanics," with its insistence on nothing more than standardized grammar and spelling, the abolition of open classrooms and audio-visual techniques, or the denigration of ethnic and dialectic modes of expression—I do not wish to reject, out of hand, the hard-won (though often excessive) victories of the sixties. Too often the discussion of literacy and writing skills is reduced to a false choice between linguistic freedom (a code term for political liberalism) and correctness (a conservatism that ostensibly masks racism, elitism, and arbitrary admissions quotas), when we know that much of the great American writing (whether in the hands of Melville and Twain; the local colorists; Hemingway and Faulkner; Ellison, Baldwin, Mailer, and Bellow; or many contemporary journalists) is an intricate fusion of the two.[5] A document of moderation and common sense in the use of language is needed. Like many documents of this sort, it may ultimately be ideal and unrealistic for a particular teacher in a particular sit-

[5] An interesting and well-reasoned article on this subject, "The Politics of Back-to-Basics," by Joan Baum, appears in *Change*, November 1976, pp. 32–36.

uation, but it will serve as an objective standard for the profession—it will give clarity to what educators ought to be accomplishing at different stages in the linguistic development of the student.

For the act of writing, of composition, is a fundamental act of education. Short-answer tests or oral reports or group projects—however valuable they obviously may be at times—do not engage the reader in the solitude of his own mind, through which he must create order and coherence on passing perceptions, on miscellaneous information. I do not believe a teacher really knows—in any subject—what his student is thinking until he examines the student's own words, his own re-creation of the subject.

Let us go further—we must go deeper—and define the need for writing in this oral, visual, aural age when one's attention is constantly diverted. Why all this concentration upon writing? Because writing is closely related to thinking: to write, the student must sort and arrange ideas, define terms, explain concepts, draw and support conclusions, gather and evaluate data. Because stress on writing results in the striking improvement of related language skills in reading, speech, and listening. Because writing is creative and the writer is active: in a multimedia world that has turned most of us into receivers of messages, there is a great need to develop active language skills. Because writing is personal and becomes a discovery of the self—the simple, separate person—in a depersonalized, machine-controlled world in which fewer and fewer people deliver messages, and the chief form of communication is a computer that sends out signals. Because writing is practical in a competitive, pragmatic society that demands skills. For all these reasons, to say nothing of the aesthetic pleasure involved in language masterfully expressed or the democratic necessity of a literate citizenry, writing—precise writing—is a fundamental act of education. And the development of a sequential curriculum in writing—without becoming inflexible—will not only raise the significance of language skills to a national consciousness: it will give some order to a discipline that has lost its discipline.

III

The third lesson of Open Admissions involves a far more extensive use of summers than has ever been made by urban schools and colleges. Our own model at The City College was modest, but it proved to be sufficiently successful during three separate summers to warrant considerable expansion.[6] We brought together teachers from local schools that shared a common pool of students: an elementary school teacher taught sixth-graders; a junior high school teacher ninth-graders, a secondary school teacher eleventh-graders. The City College instructor taught high school graduates who were entering the col-

[6] Louise Roberts, Professor of English at The City College, was the administrative leader of the summer writing camp; she formulated the particulars of the teacher-fellowship program that I have described and implemented them with great efficiency. The work of these three separate summers was successful largely because of her energies and intense dedication.

lege in the fall. Each of these schools was within the same district; each of them would ultimately be sending students to The City College. We operated a summer writing camp of 100 students at the college with four "master" teachers, each of whom had a modest fellowship for his summer teaching as well as for work before and after the summer, when he carried on his activities within his home school. This experiment was carefully controlled because initially we wanted to make certain our hypotheses would prove correct, and then, once the hypotheses did prove to be correct, it was unfortunately controlled because there were insufficient funds; but it was the first step toward a full teacher-fellowship program.

For a seven-week period, in July and August, teachers and students met four days a week, four hours a day, in an intensive language immersion program. In the afternoons there was sports recreation—swimming, baseball, basketball—as well as trips to museums and theaters and parks. During the mornings, each of the teachers met with approximately twenty-five students, who learned to listen, to take notes, to prepare for examinations, to discuss their materials in class—although, obviously, at the earlier levels of education the atmosphere was more open and relaxed. The students at each level of instruction were required to write a paper every day, which was corrected every day by a group of trained college tutors. Thus students followed a daily program that included five activities: listening, reading, writing, speaking, and tutoring—all unified by a theme topic for the day. The secondary school students listened to brief lectures and wrote assignments that ranged from American history to biology, from elementary economics to art history: they were given a simulated college atmosphere.

As outlined in the teacher-fellowship program, the four teachers involved had intensive planning sessions before the summer began, met regularly during the summer writing program, and had post-evaluations during the following fall as they continued to study the progress of the students in their home schools. A team of outside observers noted in their own independent evaluation report that the progress of the 100 students, from the initial diagnostic writing sample to the final written essay, seven weeks later, was remarkable—largely because of the close supervision and the constant revision of their work that the students were required to make. Most of the students advanced several grade levels in their writing and reading competence by the end of the seven-week summer writing camp.

The human dimensions of the summer writing program should not be lost in this record, for they represent its real meaning. The hundreds of completed essays that I have before me express emotions sufficient to make any educator pause before he speaks too harshly about the negative effects of Open Admissions. One needs to remember the eyes and voices of these children, for without them any set of academic recommendations remains utterly sterile, even pointless, and criticism becomes an easy game to play.

Imagine a workshop at eight o'clock of a hot summer

morning in an old Gothic building called Shepard Hall that is not air-conditioned. Imagine youngsters who live some distance from the building walking with their parents because they cannot afford the subway fare. Imagine a high school student collecting duplicates of the work sheets and sitting with his mother, father, brothers, and sisters around a kitchen table in the barrio, all of them struggling with the same work. Imagine a high school girl arriving in the morning, afraid that if her husband discovers she is going to school, "he'll beat me up"; or another young girl, doing very well as a writer, who cannot complete the workshop because the night before she hit her husband with a Coke bottle and he is expected to die and she is afraid she might have to go to jail; or a tenth-grader who arrives on the second day of the workshop and asks permission for her sister to "sit in," a girl who then brings a brother, then two younger sisters, until nine from the family have come; or a sixth-grader who writes about the exciting morning "when a letter came to my apartment, with my name on it, asking me to go to a writing camp." The boy finally has a chance to enter that "castle on the hill"—Shepard Hall—which is so near his home and which he has walked by on his way to school every day. Now he can enter the castle.

The assignment that reveals the deepest degree of humanity in these children is a simple one: "What would you do if you won the lottery of $50,000?"

From the elementary school students:

"I would make sure everyone in my family had a nice funeral. . . . I would buy the most expensive shoes I can find for my mother and father and sisters and brothers and grandparents and aunts and uncles. . . . I would buy pink walls, red carpets, gold lights, and white statues and then get two huge German shepherd dogs to guard the doors. . . . I would put my money in a bank and wait for the stores to open. I would begin early in the morning and I would buy and buy and buy and buy. When the money ran out, I would get more from the bank and buy and buy again."

From the high school students:

"I would buy a home. A big roomy place with a garden is my mother's fondest dream. Just thinking about it brings to mind a vision of my mother growing roses all over the place. She may well be the only woman in Harlem who has grown roses as big as grapefruit in an old wash tub. . . . I would get my mother the roses I owe her for all the Mother's day in the past. . . . I would give it all to my mother for all she does for us and my father, who's an alcoholic. She's stay with my father for twenty-five years, who's been drinking ever since. But her love is too big to describe. . . . My parents live far away in a cold unfinished house. My father has a disease for which there is no cure. Even the money would not make him healthy. But it would buy them a stove that would make it easier to go through the damp and chill Dalmatian winters. . . . I would send my brother to Oxford because he is bright and would like to study. This university has a high standing throut the world for refining some of the greatest scholars. . . . I would built an agricultural school for people to learn to produce food. I would have to remember the poor in the street in Haiti, with skinny arms and legs and swollen stomachs. There would be no more poor people on their knees begging for food. . . . I would build hospitals so that so many poor people did not have to die because they could not pay for a cure for a curable disease. If to be rich is to be blind to the miseries of the world, I will never be rich. . . . Most of all I would like a place to live for my family so that we could each have a corner of our own. Now I share a room with four brothers and sisters. We keep it neat, for we each have a shopping bag at the foot of our cot to hold our things. And we use the room in a sharing way. On one day we stay out so that my brother can practice his music. On Tuesday the room is mine, that is when I paint. But to have space every day would be wonderful. . . . I would use the money to make my grandparents secure to keep them out of a nursing home. Then they would not be lonely and forgotten. They would regain their position of elders with good advice gained through experience. . . . I would move my parents where they can live in peace. I say peace because we have never had a peaceful life in Harlem. Always the fighting and the sirens wake us up. I would find a place where we wouldn't be so close to our neighbors windows. In the summer in the heat, when the windows are open, we have to sleep with our clothes on, because we are so close to the next apartment."

Several comments should be made regarding this summer writing camp. The students volunteered for the program and were therefore self-selected and ideally motivated; their attendance record was extraordinary. Second, the students gained a sense of general confidence as they became more secure writers. This was particularly evident among the older students—in addition to discovering their own written voice, they grew to know the way a college functions without feeling the pressures of the intense academic year, and when they entered as freshmen, their confidence encouraged them to succeed in all of their subjects. In this sense, it was important to have the summer writing camp at the college—the campus itself lent prestige to the students' efforts and removed the stigma associated with a program meant to develop "remedial" skills the young people lacked. The students "graduated" with "certificates"; some won prizes for the best essays, poems, and stories. As one watched the film that our college students made of the program, one realized the possibilities of the summer writing camp: student after student read his final essay, thanking all of us for helping and for making his summer profitable.[7] There is no reason why a summer program of this sort cannot be located in every urban college or high school, no reason why students cannot be given intensive writing

[7] Equally poignant was the appearance each morning of mothers who left their elementary school children in class and then went to work. So many of these mothers told me, toward the end of the summer writing program, how much they themselves would like to participate in this kind of workshop. In part the reason was to improve their own skills, to better themselves; but the deeper reason, as several women confessed, was that they feared their children might one day be ashamed of them.

It would seem that a city college, as part of the general policy of Open Admissions, should offer writing courses for adults in the evenings and on weekends—and, as I later suggest, through the medium of television.

instruction during the summer before they enter college. With success, intensive summer work in writing will at least partially release the normal school and college programs from their heavy and expensive burden of remediation.

The last important comment that should be made about the summer writing camp has to do with the use of trained college tutors. The programs could never have been successful without these gifted undergraduates who were majoring in English and history and political science —indeed every subject in the curriculum—and who earned a modest stipend for their summer work. But this use of tutors goes far beyond the summer writing program and really constitutes the fourth lesson that Open Admissions offered me.

IV

This lesson stems from my realization that no school teacher, however conscientious, can carry on five classes, each with thirty-five students, and correct the student papers with the care they require. The most diligent teacher, even in a high school with few disciplinary problems, must struggle to keep up with different preparations every day as well as with the endless records that a highly bureaucratized school system demands. The expectation that a teacher will correct 175 papers regularly and thoroughly is simply unrealistic. Yet we continue with that expectation and the essays are either not assigned or are superficially corrected—and the student rarely meets with the teacher in the personal conference through which writing is most effectively improved. There have been many suggestions of how to alleviate this condition which exists in every classroom of America—students correcting each others' papers, computer-assisted instruction—and I do not pretend there is a simple answer or any single answer; but of all the efforts that I have personally witnessed, the most promising is the use of college tutors as assistants to classroom teachers.

If we really mean to cure the national disease of illiteracy, we need to develop an urban corps of college tutors that will be as vital as the Peace Corps. The tutors must first be trained in classes that deal with formal grammar and syntax as well as with the specific problems of language and dialect they will encounter in the tutoring relationship; they must learn to write well so that they can teach others, and they must learn how to read and judge student papers. At the same time, the tutors must be given guidance in learning theory and adolescent psychology—by faculty in the liberal arts as well as in the School of Education—so that their personal relations with students are as reinforcing as possible. Once the college tutor is "trained," he can then be assigned to assist the classroom teacher at the appropriate level of education and conduct individual or group tutorials with three, four, or five students before or after school—whenever the schedule of the school allows—so that the writing of students will be corrected far more frequently than is presently possible.

These four lessons of Open Admissions are fundamental to any synthesis for the humanities. There is no simple solution to illiteracy, but if extraordinary efforts are not made at this level, the humanities will be reserved for too few people. These lessons imply a fifth—a sequential study of literature that parallels the study of writing.[8]

V

As in the case of composition, a fellowship program, a summer institute, and the use of college tutors can improve the teaching of literature markedly. There has been a historical and harmful separation between the theoretical considerations of literature in graduate school and the actual discussion of texts in the classroom. The victims have been the students. In a time when fewer young people are entering the profession of teaching and thus bringing with them the newest developments in research

[8] My observations regarding a sequential study of literature owe a great deal to the participants of a pre-convention conference, sponsored by the Commission on Literature when I was its director, at the 1975 convention of the National Council of Teachers of English: Bruce Appleby (Southern Illinois University), Richard Barksdale (University of Illinois), Lydia Bronte (Rockefeller Foundation), Arthur Eastman (Virginia Polytechnic University), Sam Erskine (Ginn and Company), Edmund Farrell (University of Texas at Austin), Harry Finestone (University of California, Northridge), John Gerber (SUNY Albany), George Gerbner (Annenberg School of Communications, University of Pennsylvania), Robert Spencer Johnson (Alberston Junior High School), Richard Manatt (St. Martin's Press), Norine Odland (University of Minnesota), Roy Harvey Pearce (University of California, San Diego), Bette Peltola (University of Wisconsin), Edward Quinn (The City College of New York), Helen Renthal (School Librarian), James Squire (Ginn and Company), Caroline Shrodes (San Francisco University), Adele Stern (Paramus Schools, New Jersey), Betty True (School Librarian, Robbinsdale, Minnesota), and Darwin Turner (University of Iowa).

and pedagogy, the retraining of current instructors—from first grade through college—is essential. That retraining should be sponsored by post-graduate programs of literature, in co-operation with Schools of Education.

Nowhere in the curriculum is a synthesis of learning—in theory and pedagogy—more essential than in the reading of poetry, fiction, drama, and the various forms of discursive prose. The study of literature in American schools and colleges now suffers from a fragmentation of approach which leads to duplication and confusion. The multiple elective system so prevalent in secondary schools has helped to revive interest in many aspects of literature, but it has blurred an incremental pattern upon which teachers and students throughout the system can depend. Furthermore, the use of anthologies and "readers"—from grade school throughout college—has created a sensibility trained to read *The Reader's Digest* rather than whole books. So much of our culture in the schools is filtered through excerpts or review guides that isolate "the main idea." The pleasure of reading the entire book an author has created has been lost, and with it the pleasure of reading itself is gone. We have concentrated so heavily on "how" to read and on the packaging of books that we have too often forgotten "what" we offer students; our devotion to skills has obscured the enjoyment of reading.

A central question in any sequential study of literature is the identification of those relationships the teacher must establish between the highly saturated symbolic structure in the mind of the student who has watched a great deal of television and the special critical skills, joys, and values derived from reading. The skills and values acquired from the study of literature can clearly be adapted to the watching of television drama and documentary. But it is essential that the teacher realize he can no longer ignore or be condescending to television—it has become, in George Gerbner's phrase, the religion of America. For the first time in human history children are watching the behavior of parents who themselves were indoctrinated into television. The parents often find pleasure in watching television rather than in reading, even when they urge their children to study. It is no wonder that the children see reading as a chore and associate it exclusively with "verbal scores" and skills and tests—with all the negative aspects of school.

The teacher must find ways of developing courses in comparative media that will allow the study of books to illuminate the enormous amount of television viewing which occurs in the lives of most Americans as well as to support the traditional purposes of literature itself. Of equal importance, careful reading must provide the student with a sharp critical awareness so that he can measure the mediocrity or excellence of a soap opera, the superficiality or thoroughness of a news analysis, the bias of a documentary—as he would in reading print journalism or any written form of literature. On one hand, the teacher needs to integrate presentations of drama, ballet, and music with textual study; on the other hand, he must make the student so alert a critic of the media that as a future viewer (or practitioner) he will be highly selective in his use of television and film, insisting upon the most rigorous standards in his entertainment, his news, his literature.

Television and film will only be as complex and sophisticated as the viewers themselves—but they will be nothing more than popular entertainment, and the lowest form of entertainment, if teachers of literature consider them with only disdain. We study the popular literature of the past to learn the mores and habits of common people; television is our popular literature, and we need to bring to it full knowledge, full discrimination. The primacy of the written word has diminished and teachers of literature must understand the full implications of that fact. A critical, analytical, and discriminating approach to the *total* symbolic environment has become a necessity in mass-produced cultures. Indeed the teacher who does not include television in his treatment of literature generally—analyzing actual programs in the way he analyzes fiction, poetry, and the essay—is simply not confronting that mode of communication, imaginative and reportorial, that has shaped much of his student's thinking.

In considering any "sequential" development of the study of literature, the following aspects of the educational process—from pre-school to college—should occur simultaneously:

1. A stress on the *internal response* to literature.

2. The relationship of literary study *to the psychological development and growth of the child*. More thinking (and consultation with professional psychologists) must be done in regard to when in his development the child reads a particular work of literature.

3. *The development of skills* in language (the ability to interpret products of the fictive imagination with precision and perception).

4. The constant relationship between different forms of media.

With these broad goals as shaping forces in the study of literature, the development of certain skills may be recommended at different stages of the student's growth.

In the pre-school period (ages two to five), the storytelling or narrative power should be developed. Poetry should be read aloud, thus developing the lyric response, and the child should *listen* to language. At this age especially the personal response is significant; formal judgments should be avoided so that musical patterns, relationships of the visual to the written word, the sound of poetry may be stressed. The sheer pleasure of reading needs to be encouraged by those teachers who read aloud well.[9]

[9] The parents are the ideal first teachers who can shape positive attitudes toward learning. The extent to which educators in nursery and elementary school can persuade parents of pre-schoolers to participate in these first stages of reading will largely determine the child's success in school.

One program that addresses itself to this fundamental problem is "Failsafe," in the Houston public school system. The "statement of need" reads as follows: "Based on the factors which affect education today—knowledge explosion, societal demands for the teaching of more subjects, and mobility of population, it will be difficult to move toward the expectations of parents unless the home assumes a larger role in direct instructional support of the teacher in the classroom. Learning is not a six hour activity but one which continues throughout the waking day." An elaborate kit is given to the parents, which contains specific advice on how to make learning enjoyable for the pre-schooler and recommends strategies for bringing the parent into the education of his child.

Another program, more national in scope, is "Reading is Fundamental." Mrs. Robert McNamara, chairman of this important effort, has stressed

From the ages of five through seven, certain interpretative skills may be introduced: style; tone; point of view; plot structure; characterization. Comparative media —television and film—should be used as bridges to the written word. In this period when reading is developed as a specific skill, its enjoyment should not be sacrificed at the expense of developing the skill. The book as an object seems especially important to the child—the first book many of them will actually handle and take home—and it should be associated with excitement, adventure, and pleasure. This period is critical in terms of establishing certain sympathetic patterns and attitudes, and it needs further exploration. Certain questions are vexing: should the skill of reading be separated from the enjoyment and "play" of reading—or should reading skills and the enjoyment of reading literature be interwoven? Educators have divided opinions, which suggests the need for further study, but most agree that too often the act of learning to read is associated with pain and work and discourages a self-determined reading experience on the part of the student. At this age, as well as at earlier and later stages, the written response to literature should be developed. This might take at least two forms: the ordered response of composition—i.e., the student's interpretation of works of art—and the student's own imaginative creation.

---

the need for parental involvement. "Reading should be fun," she has remarked, and urges that the subject matter of books be directed to the personal interests of children, whether they are from Appalachia, the inner city, or the Southwest, rather than be imposed upon them externally. She also underscores the need for "pride of ownership," and has helped to develop 1,000 programs which have 5 million books for 1 million children.

Then, from the ages of seven through twelve, literary terminology may be introduced—concepts of tragedy, comedy, myth, folklore, genre, legend, author's intent, tone, style, voice, structure, and flashback. In the secondary school and college these interpretative skills should be further refined; the response to literature intensified; language skills developed as the student gives ordered response to the literature he reads.

These are some of the primary objectives of the study of literature, and they depend upon the accumulation of skills we can designate at different points along a continuum in the study of the humanities that stretches from pre-school through college. Teachers of literature and mass media are at a turning point. It is clear, as various commentators have indicated, that the humanities are threatened by a variety of forces: vocationalism, the devaluation of the past, the debasement of language, the decline of reading imaginative literature as a force in the lives of most Americans. The kind of sequential study of literature that I have suggested goes far beyond my competence. A distinguished task force of humanists, sponsored by an organization like the National Endowment for the Humanities, should accumulate the data and current research regarding a variety of critical questions: What is the actual role of television in the imaginative lives of students? To what extent should courses in television viewing be integrated into the curriculum of literature? What is the relationship of the mass media to the reading habits of students? How much do students read outside of school? What do they actually read? What attitudes do they bring to the reading experience? What kinds of literary theory can be most readily adapted to the classroom? My own views rest upon two principles: the future of the humanities will depend on applying the traditional humanistic skills to mass communications so that a future curriculum of literature will include the study of comparative media; and, second, the relationship between literary theory, as promulgated in graduate schools, and the teaching of literature, as practiced in the classroom, has to be more closely connected.

Within this broad perspective, I believe in settling upon certain great works—as few as possible—that illustrate the skills one wishes to develop. One should heed Thoreau's admonition, especially in view of the atomized curricula everywhere in American education: "You had better read the best books first or you may never read them at all." Teachers at subsequent levels of education must be able to take for granted the student's acquisition of fundamental skills in writing and reading as well as of a common body of knowledge—otherwise, the curriculum loses a clear sense of purpose for both teacher and student. Humanists can never develop a curriculum resembling that of mathematics in which a sequential hierarchy of skills and knowledge is essential and clear. But the curriculum can certainly be redeemed from its current chaos; it need not lack any sequence at all.

In stressing the need to develop a sequential study of language and literature, I do not mean to minimize the significance of integrated learning and interdisciplinary study at every stage of education. The language arts of writing, reading, listening, and speaking should reinforce one another at the remedial as well as at the most sophisticated levels of learning. Literature should be studied in the interdisciplinary context of history, art, philosophy, religion, political science, and sociology—otherwise, it will be little more than a development of interpretative skills whose informing principle is only the close reading of the text.

In terms of education and the development of a basis for any core curriculum or future for the humanities, the improvement of language skills, addressed in these first five lessons, is essential. This means working with our colleagues at earlier levels of education. This means teacher training during the academic year and the support of college tutors for these classroom teachers; this means intensive summer writing programs before students enter college; this means developing curricular materials that are shared with others in the school system and a research unit that draws together the best thinking about the problems of language acquisition; this means the establishment of a National Center for Literacy, with urban branches throughout the country, that can serve pragmatically the school children of America. We have a National Endowment for the Humanities and a National Endowment for the Arts, but the national center that is truly critical for the survival of our democracy is one that must concentrate on literacy. There is a challenge to a senator like Hayakawa or Moynihan—to cite only two most closely identified with "language in thought and action" or a society "beyond the melting pot"; there is a challenge for federal funds, through federal legislation.

The core curriculum that I will now suggest—my sixth lesson of Open Admissions—depends upon a total commitment to curing the disease of illiteracy. Without this commitment, any design of a college curriculum, however cogent it may be, will be hollow, will remain nothing but a set of paper intentions.

In all that I have written regarding a sequential study of language and literature, I am aware of how particularly difficult implementation is in urban schools where the future Open Admissions student learns, where language problems are so fundamental, truancy a frequent problem, discipline the dissonant music of each lesson. I think I know the practical difficulties in these classrooms, yet I can only state my ideas in a rather "pure" form if they are to be useful at all. And this applies particularly to my sixth lesson of Open Admissions, a lesson that draws together much of what I have said: the necessity of a core curriculum in the first year of a student's college education.

VI

The first year of a college education must be tightly structured and articulated. Students need to pursue a course of study with clearly stated educational goals in the humanities, social sciences, and sciences that develop sophisticated communications skills:

1. The ability to argue and interpret persuasively so

that the study of inductive and deductive reasoning as well as cause and effect relationships leads to a knowledge of the general principles of logic.

2. The development of writing skills that include a developed familiarity with comparison and contrast, description, and summary—techniques that will train the student in the marshaling of evidence and that will ultimately help him in the preparation of a simple research paper.

3. The acquisition of a facility in speech—the liberation of the student's own voice—that focuses upon techniques of argumentation and presentation.

4. An understanding of scientific attitudes, of scientific processes, of the means by which scientific material is collected and interpreted, of ways hypotheses are formulated from available data and predictions made, and of science as a human endeavor with social consequences.

5. A familiarity with the library and its intelligent use.[10]

6. A basic knowledge of the computer that would include, for example, methods of information storage and retrieval.

The clarification of these intentions is essential—especially in an age when the content of the curriculum will shift as it mirrors the expanding knowledge of the

[10] In a time when the sources of information are more and more concentrated in fewer and fewer people—with all the dangers to a democracy that may result from this tendency—the resources of the library cannot be stressed enough. For journalists, especially, the need to do one's own research and arrive at one's own perspective before receiving the press releases or public relations of a community organization, state government, or foreign power is crucial.

world, especially when we must respond to a technological age in which the visual representation of life—in
television and film—forms the image of reality for most
students. But however we relate the visual and aural
modes of communication to the written word, we need to
know the intentions of the core curriculum—these will not
change fundamentally—so that they can be integrated
with whatever content we consider significant. Organically fused, intent and content will then serve as an
introduction to the broad fields of concentration the student will pursue in his later college years.

1. Certainly any core curriculum pertinent to the needs
of modern society must include the study of language and
modern communications, literature, and the arts; world
civilization and culture; the individual and his kinship to
society; political economy; the biological and physical sciences. At the same time, as the student pursues this core
curriculum, he should be required to take a seminar that
develops critical skills in reading, analysis, and research.

2. Writing must be an integral element in the core curriculum. Instructors need to attend workshops for realizing writing objectives and they should be held accountable for this fundamental charge. A year of freshman
English—distinct from remedial work in writing—and one
semester of speech should be assigned to all students during the period they are engaged in the courses of the
core curriculum. Most importantly, these "skills" courses
should be organically related in every way to those of
"content": the essay topics assigned in freshman English

should be drawn, wherever possible, from the students' other subjects.

3. Throughout this one-year period, curriculum guidance must be greatly intensified. One of the severest problems for the underprepared student, especially, is the unrealistic expectation he often sets for himself. The student who has deep remedial needs in arithmetic and algebra sees himself as a physician; the student who can scarcely express himself wants to be a journalist. These dreams are implicitly accepted by the sincere teacher who naturally struggles to help a student succeed, whatever his preparation may be; but the idealism of Open Admissions, so American in its impulse, cannot be debased into a sentimentality that is ultimately unfair to the student himself. It has to be tempered by a pragmatism equally American, and the goals of the student must be adjusted to his talents.

A pamphlet needs to be produced that defines the first year of college work in institutions committed to Open Admissions: the goals expected of students; the minimal knowledge to be acquired by the end of the core curriculum; the basic skills essential to study for upper-level work. The pamphlet should be distributed to secondary schools so that teachers and students know what is expected of them, know what is meant when one speaks of the core of a liberal arts education. If a freshman program could be so designed, individual departments would then develop major fields of study for students who share a common body of knowledge and a common set of aptitudes. And secondary schools would have a clear sense of how to shape their own curricula.

In making these recommendations concerning the core curriculum, I am aware of how difficult it is to implement them practically, given the academic politics of most institutions. For more than three years, I sat at the long table on the second floor of our administration building and listened to the specific arguments of departmental representatives in defense of their individual disciplines at the same time as they agreed abstractly that a coherent core curriculum was desirable. There are legitimate points of disagreement between educators like me who feel that an interdisciplinary core curriculum is feasible and those who claim that such an approach inevitably debases a specific discipline, which must be introduced from its unique perspective with its special vocabulary and dimensions.

But there are also many administrative and structural forces that work so heavily against curricular coherence, we can scarcely count the ways. The survival of departments depends upon the popularity of their elective courses so that each faculty member drawn into the teaching of core courses is viewed as a loss to the preservation of his discipline, his department. The reward system at most colleges is rooted in publications that will lend national prestige to the institution, and faculty—including those who no longer wish to write or do research—respond accordingly. They know that the publication of an article in an academic journal will carry far more credit than the distribution of an internal document, however excellent the local report may be, however much it will improve the actual operation of the institution. Then there is the teaching itself. Faculty often view the instruction of freshmen as having the least status for themselves. They also know that work in core courses involves interdisciplinary efforts which run counter to their own training in graduate school and demands classroom preparation that will prevent them from developing a body of work calculated to advance their careers within their own disciplines. Finally, they naturally want to be stimulated toward this writing by working with sophisticated students in their fields. These forces are powerful to varying degrees within individual colleges and are controlled by the profession at large. One is known, almost exclusively in academic life, by one's publications: that is the reality behind the rhetoric of our profession.

In order to make the core curriculum a true value for faculty as well as for students, the administration of a college must support instructors engaged in its development —the quality of this kind of educational planning has to be measured as seriously as external publication and has to be rewarded (or not rewarded) accordingly. Second, the most distinguished faculty should be drawn into the development and teaching of a core curriculum so that it becomes a matter of prestige for younger instructors to serve on the planning committee and ultimately to teach the courses themselves. Third, all departmental credit should be eliminated from the core so that no department feels it must have a representative course through which credit is generated; this will remove a good deal of the ac-

ademic politics from curriculum design and free everyone
to think about the curriculum and not about protecting
his constituency. Finally, in addition to preparing a pamphlet that defines the aims and purposes of the core curriculum, a text of readings should be designed that will
reflect the range of core subjects. Because of the need to
stress composition—especially in colleges committed to
Open Admissions—this text should be conditioned by
written assignments and rhetorical exercises directly
linked to language study in freshman composition and in
the core courses themselves.

Beyond the need for curricular coherence and genuine
administrative support of the core curriculum, there is
one element absent from all these remarks, without which
the whole enterprise is doomed—an element so central it
will be assumed or forgotten if I do not state it. My suggestions may be more or less correct and certainly can be
made more comprehensive and precise, but they are use-
less without the magic of the classroom: the individual
student learning of human possibility and alien lives, of
responding personally to the conflict in character or the
power of language, to the wonder of a scientific discovery
or experiment, to the excitement of a philosophical mind,
to the creative impulse in ballet and art and drama and
music that so charges his own sensibility he wants to
create the world anew. No set of recommendations, however elegant, can replace what Wordsworth called the
splendor in the grass, the glory in the flower; only a
teacher or an artist can help the student take the journey
inward so that he can emerge from his own creativity,

which is after all his sense of power, to formal analysis and ordered response, to a composition of the mind.

We know that our students want to create. We see their intense interest in what we call "creative" writing, in performing and fine arts; we see their active wish to become journalists or lawyers or doctors—to do as well as study, to shape as well as be shaped. And though, unfortunately, this impulse too often takes the form of nothing more than vocational training, it can lead to an organic and intensely meaningful study of the humanities because then the student knows, as Valéry once said of reading, that he is learning for some quite personal purpose.

This sense of purpose is most difficult to establish in the study of foreign languages—an aspect of the curriculum crucial to a future for the humanities. The significance of understanding a culture other than one's own need scarcely be stressed in a multi-lingual world shrunk by modern technology, and the language of a people provides the fundamental clue to the texture of its living. We understand this truism and we try to persuade our students of it, but they struggle with the linguistic currency of this country as well as with the specialized language of their future profession, and they doubt that they can come even close to mastery of a foreign language within one or two years. Indeed, how often have humanists heard these questions from their colleagues in the sciences, social sciences, and professional schools: Should a competence in foreign languages really be required of all students? Can we afford to maintain classical languages like Greek, Latin, and Hebrew in the curriculum? What should be the proper relationship of foreign language instruction to the rest of the curriculum? Sometimes, humanists even ask these questions of themselves. They are difficult questions under any circumstances, but in a college committed to Open Admissions, they seem almost insoluble. I have struggled toward my own rather modest solutions, and I offer them as my seventh lesson of Open Admissions.

VII

When I became Dean of Humanities, there were at least fifteen languages offered at The City College: Arabic, Chinese (Mandarin and Cantonese), French, German, Greek, Hebrew, Italian, Japanese, Latin, Portuguese, Spanish, Russian, Sanskrit, Swahili, and Yiddish. Except for Spanish and to some degree French, where foreign-born Hispanics and Haitians took courses in their native tongue, the other language programs offered almost entirely elementary work. Sophisticated literature, when it was studied at all, was read in English.

The enrollment in foreign languages declined precipitously during Open Admissions—especially in Greek, Latin, Hebrew, and Russian—and it soon seemed that these languages were no longer administratively—i.e., economically—defensible. Still one could not sacrifice the languages entirely, however much Open Admissions made them seem irrelevant, even at times quixotic. One knew what one would be sacrificing if one seized the easy economical solutions—the final solutions. These languages lay

at the foundation of Western civilization and represented
the cultures of the world—one had to hold on, in the hope
that student interest would increase; one had to hold on,
even if only a handful of students wanted to study Vergil
and Homer and Goethe and Tolstoy in the original; one
had to support these languages if the college was to be
something more than an instrument of expediency. . . .
Even for a handful of students one had to hold on, for the
study of foreign languages represented an important intellectual meaning to the most remedial of students on the
same campus, students who might themselves never study
Greek or Latin, Hebrew, Russian, or Chinese, but who
needed to know that these languages and their cultures
existed for their younger brothers and sisters, for their
children, for their own legacy.

But how could one hold on?

One way of maintaining an interest in foreign languages is through the development of a strong world literature program in English whose foundation course is in
the core curriculum. Only by a fascination with the culture of a foreign country will the student want to know its
language. Another is through the use of comparative
media to enhance the written word: films, recordings, television productions, theater, dance, and music. The revival of interest in classical culture, particularly, can be
most imaginatively developed through the performing arts
—and I will have more to say about this interaction as I
discuss the significance of the arts to the future of the
humanities. Finally, faculties in foreign languages must
develop concentrations or options for students who are

majoring in business, engineering, or other professional subjects. Often students are controlled by the required subjects of their professional training, but this is not always the case. Most accreditation associations insist upon a certain percentage of courses in the liberal arts—the American Assembly of Collegiate Schools of Business requires 40 per cent, the Engineers Council for Professional Development, 20 per cent—and the deans of professional schools, at least in my experience, are eager for interdisciplinary programs in the humanities to enhance their curriculum: they do not want to train technicians. Some of the most attractive positions that result from professional education may already be found in foreign countries—certainly in underdeveloped nations. A French, Spanish, or Chinese option that not only is rooted in language training but also offers an interdisciplinary approach to the culture should be attractive indeed to career-oriented students who want to go beyond pragmatic training and enter into a profession.

In perpetuating the study of languages that may be temporarily unpopular but that must be kept in the curriculum, individual and group tutorials should be offered at whatever level of sophistication the student can sustain; the tutorials will be appropriately "counted" as part of the faculty work load, and the students will be fortunate enough to enjoy a form of instruction that has flourished for British students for many years. I do not minimize the expense of this kind of arrangement. But the university, if it is to be a university, must support the study of foreign languages, even though it may be a financial liability; at the same time, the faculty of foreign languages must reduce that liability, insofar as possible, by recognizing that a tutorial program of the kind I recommend will mean greater work for them. If they want to have courses in Catullus and Horace that enroll only three or four students, they must be willing to accept such courses as group tutorials and, in order to fill out their programs, assume a work load in English as a Second Language or composition.

The faculty of foreign languages must be persuaded to take a leadership role in whatever program of English as a Second Language exists at the college. Those foreign-born students who need remediation in English can be encouraged to pursue their native culture at a more advanced level: high literacy in a native language like Spanish, French, or Chinese will enhance functional literacy in English.

In many urban institutions this work is no small matter. At The City College of New York, for example, more than 20 per cent of the student body now speaks English as a second language, and statistics suggest that this trend will continue at the same time as the general pool of students diminishes. As a report recently issued by the State Education Department of New York indicates, there will be a "28 per cent decline in the number of students who will graduate from New York City high schools in the next decade . . . the City University of New York will have to prepare for the influx of most of these students into the system's community colleges and four-year institutions . . . the primary mission of the university will have to change to meet the need of black and Hispanic students, many of whom will require special remedial help. . . . Somehow, postsecondary institutions will have to bridge the gap between students who are increasingly drawn from poor, immigrant, non-English speaking, educationally disadvantaged groups and a job market in which an increasing proportion of openings will require a full four-year college education at a minimum."

As English faculties have had to concentrate their energies on the remedial instruction of native-born students, foreign language teachers need to turn their talents to helping the foreign-born. In those colleges where few English as a Second Language students are present, "underemployed" foreign language instructors will have to be retrained to teach English. The close contact of conference work in English composition courses provides a rare opportunity to lead students into more sophisticated work in the humanities. Retreating to one's discipline—whether it is the teaching of medieval English or eighteenth-century Spanish literature—will only place the faculty in the position of some classicists who have not made sufficient bridges with contemporary culture: it is finally self-destructive. One can view language training as nothing but a burden that is in constant conflict with the study of literature, or one can see it as the foundation to a world literature program, even if it is a rather elementary one. . . . I know the compromises implicit in these recommendations —the gap between one's scholarship and one's teaching, between one's original idea of a career and the career itself; but one has no choice any longer—if a career is to be pursued at all—and one must not only believe in the need for foreign language study, one must sacrifice to sustain that need, even in these parlous times.[11]

Competence in a language other than English would seem the least to require of a college student entering our "global village." His instruction should emphasize the spoken language, wherever possible, in the form of the "Ulpan" or of "total immersion" in the language, so that he has the sense of personal accomplishment—not to speak of sheer fun—that can come most dramatically in studying foreign languages. There is no reason why students cannot be brought to a level of minimum spoken and written competence in one of the modern languages before they graduate from college. Such competence is one safeguard against a tendency toward parochialism and narrow nationalism in the curriculum and our culture generally. It is a requirement that represents a value for every future engineer or architect or businessman—for anyone who hopes to move into a managerial position that will require interaction with cultures other than his own.[12]

[11] All of these recommendations, I should add, are made with the assumption that tenure will not be violated.

[12] In large metropolitan areas, the possibility of a program for translators can be pursued. There are many organizations that need people fluent in at least two foreign languages: multi-national corporations, airlines, travel bureaus, publishing houses, newspapers, magazines. But this kind of program does depend upon a sufficient number of students with sophisticated training in the foreign culture as well as in the language skill itself. It is interesting to note that most American students fail the United Nations test for translators in "general culture" far more frequently than they do in "skills."

Probably the most effective structure that can accommodate a program for translators is continuing education. Needless to say, the presence of the program, however small, will be a constant validation of the undergraduate courses in foreign languages.

A fundamental reason why the study of foreign languages and culture generally is resisted by Open Admissions students is their intense interest in career or professional education. They want to move from remediation to the world of work directly. One can decry this reality, but that is finally an evasion, especially in colleges where students of working-class families want marketable skills and where the imposition of a highly structured curriculum—one that goes beyond "core" and basic skills—will simply drive students away.

In liberal arts colleges that attract better-prepared and more affluent students, the curriculum is predicated on the assumption that professional education will continue after undergraduate school. But at the city colleges of this country, the humanities and pre-professional education are in a very special tension; the students feel that they cannot afford to wait. Indeed, at The City College of New York that tension has threatened at times to tear apart a traditional faculty of liberal arts who have regarded with hostility an administration that has encouraged pre-professional programs because it knows enrollment (upon which the budget depends) is generated by those programs and not by liberal arts. From this dilemma emerges the eighth lesson provided by Open Admissions: the necessary connection that must be made between the humanities and pre-professional education.

VIII

The following is a description of a grant proposal that faculty representatives from economics, English, biology, psychology, and sociology developed with my associate and me.[13] There is a core curriculum that all students are required to take during their freshman year. Beyond the core and the necessary courses in remediation, students choose a pre-professional track in administration and management; or communications, mass media, and public policy; or energy, ecology, and environment; or human development; or public service. The centrality of the humanities to pre-professional training is asserted by formalizing the practice of communications skills within these various tracks, and by developing a set of readings, common to all programs, that clarify values and ethics and that give historical perspective to the contemporaneous character of pre-professional training. "The decision to focus on public policy"—so reads our newsletter to the faculty—"is the natural result of two related circumstances. First, the College is witnessing the simultaneous development of several public policy programs. Second, public policy issues are related fundamentally to issues at the heart of the humanities: the ways the past shapes the

[13] "The Humanities, Pre-professional Education, and Public Policy" is a proposal implemented in its details by Professor Saul Brody of the Department of English, The City College of New York. The quoted passages that follow are from various working documents drafted by Professor Brody, whose intelligence and administrative skills were largely responsible for the success of the senior course, "Public Policy and Human Values."

present, the ways a society develops and acts on its values, the tension between individual and societal needs."

The need to have humanistic concerns organically related to these pre-professional programs is stressed in seminars conducted for participating faculty. These seminars pose the practical difficulties of all "retraining" sessions for college instructors. Many faculty, trained as biologists or psychologists or economists, feel unqualified to be speaking "professionally" about ethics and morality; others question that values can be taught at all; still others resist any faculty seminars as an implicit criticism of their own professional competence. The professionalization of the university is very deeply entrenched—not simply in professional schools but in the academic disciplines, too, and even within the disciplines themselves, as one still hears that a seventeenth-century specialist or classicist cannot teach a course in contemporary literature because it is not his "speciality." Too often there is no college faculty but a faculty of disciplines, and on an undergraduate level this tendency to perpetuate the narrow specialization of graduate studies into an undergraduate education is particularly divisive and anti-intellectual—especially in a world where all disciplines are so obviously interactive and in a college where the education must be made as coherent as possible. These faculty seminars break down those artificial barriers that separate disciplines; and if the initial participants are volunteers, the excitement of their work will soon be shared by more recalcitrant colleagues.

The students pursuing pre-professional training, even

though it may be infused with a humanistic perspective, need to be brought together at the end of their college careers so as to place all that they have learned in the broadest possible context of public policy and human values. The special feature of the program in "The Humanities, Pre-professional Education, and Public Policy" is therefore a capstone course, taken during the senior year—a course that serves as a bridge between the student's entire undergraduate education and the world of work he soon will be entering.

My own sense of the need for this course was inspired by Theodore Hesburgh, who has accused the American university of abdicating all concern for values. "We have become so obsessed with objectivity that we have neutralized any standing for anything. The result is that we turn out highly competent but morally neutral people, the kind of people who have the sophisticated techniques required to create a Watergate, while never asking themselves the fundamental question if it is right or wrong to behave thus . . . We have managed to become so fragmented and so overspecialized as to be completely dissipated. We don't have the great questions elucidated in the youngsters' minds today, about love and hate, peace and war, violence and nonviolence, questions of humanity and inhumanity, beauty and ugliness, the kind of great sweeping global, cosmic questions that used to always be a part of a humanistic education, that involved an approach to history and literature, art, music, mathematics, science, philosophy, and theology, that is to say, a total unified mix. . . . I don't want any student to graduate from Notre Dame without being confronted with the reality of world hunger, the reality of global injustice, the need for him to make moral decisions as public servant, politician, engineer, lawyer, doctor, teacher, or priest."

These remarks are fundamental to the purposes of the contemporary American university and our attempt to implement their meaning at The City College has been through the capstone course, "Public Policy and Human Values." Although we thought originally of designing a syllabus of great books that would serve as a humanistic synthesis of all that the students had learned, we decided to associate the "great books" with the pre-professional programs and to develop a course that seemed organic to the lives the students would lead, that connected thought with action, literature with life, learning with its application. Our goals in this course were clear: we wanted "students to deal with the ethical and moral implications of the ways in which public policy is formulated and implemented," and we wanted them to read from significant texts at the same time as they came to grips with that policy. As the planning committee shaped the course and then offered it through four departments (English, biology, economics, and sociology), "Public Policy and Human Values" became "aggressively multi-disciplinary." It also offered "students the opportunity to participate in a complex, sophisticated computer simulation exercise" that bears some detailed description:

"In the exercise students assume roles central to the life of a simulated city and county called Metro-Apex. As residents of Metro-Apex, some students are city or county planners or politicians; other run industrial plants or are land developers; still others serve on an Environmental Quality Agency, or represent pressure groups, or the mass media. All these groups act upon each other as they work to reach their goals. For instance, an industrialist seeking to purchase land in order to construct a plant works with a developer in seeking a zoning variance from planners and politicians who themselves are under pressure from EQA to obtain an environmental impact statement. At the end, the computer measures the results of the decisions in terms of changed land values, employment, income, tax revenues, air and water pollution, solid waste production, housing starts, public services, public health, and a multitude of other variables.

"Through the simulation, students are given both the experience of having to determine public policy within the constraints typically imposed by inadequate time, information, and budget—and the opportunity to examine the impact of their decisions on the life of the community. Finally, and as importantly, drawing upon their experience with the simulation, required readings, and guest speakers with professional experience in roles that parallel the exercise roles, the students assess the broad ethical and philosophical dimensions of public policy formulation."

This is but one course in a complex educational design, "The Humanities, Pre-professional Education, and Public Policy"; it is not, in and of itself, the resolution to the tensions between liberal arts and professional education, nor does it pretend to be a synthesis for the humanities. But it does bring the study of the humanities into an organic relationship with professional judgments and decisions students will be forced to make later in their lives; it bridges technology, in the form of the computer, with the humanistic uses of that technology. It is one necessary element in a synthesis for the humanities.

The pre-professional programs that were part of our proposal were simply those that individual faculty members had been processing independently—we made the imaginative connections among them. Other programs can easily be adapted to this design and a capstone seminar of the sort I describe should certainly include students in engineering, architecture, biomedicine, law— in every professionalized program in the curriculum. Indeed, if possible, a seminar on "Public Policy and Human Values" ought to be required of every student at the college, during his senior year, taught by as many faculty as possible—precisely so that no student will graduate "without being confronted with the reality of world hunger, the reality of global injustice, the need for him to make moral decisions as public servant, politician, engineer, lawyer, doctor, teacher, or priest."

The one pre-professional program that bears most directly upon the study of humanities and that, in many ways, is transforming it, is mass communications—the study of print, electronic journalism, broadcasting, films, book publishing, public relations, and advertising. Not only are careers in these fields more available, not only have they increased dramatically within the past generation as a result of advancing technology, not only do they exert enormous influence on every American's life—they are the most powerful shapers of public policy in this country.

The conventional student of language and literature has been drawn toward mass communications precisely because of its dramatic power. From the enormous number of cartoons and commercials people absorb to the manipulation of the media by presidential candidates; from the latest faddish entertainment in television and newspapers and books to the daily decisions of editors about what news their public will read—the student senses that here is a more influential form of education than teaching itself. It is precisely the power of mass communications that conventional academic humanists despise and envy. At the same time they justly deplore the loss of precious values that have been hard won, over centuries and centuries of time, and that have now been replaced by the evanescent nature of rapid-fire journalism: the emphasis on slick technique rather than on content that forces one to think sharply and feel deeply; the simplification of complex materials; the concentration on superficial manner rather than on substantive matter; the domination of an advertising industry that persuades one to do no more than buy and consume, the creation of television plays that have a beginning, middle, and end and a problem that is always solved in an arbitrary time frame, thus falsifying the human condition. "The only thing easier to do than watch television," one critic has told me, "is breathe." Most frightening for any humanist is the need to appeal to huge numbers of people at the same time, with the inevitable surrender of anything grainy or difficult in the creator's art and thought. Furthermore, the concentration of communications into the hands of fewer and fewer people, who are superior technicians in how to engage the attention of a vast audience, is dangerous to all of us. The more magazines and books and individual television stations, the more messages sent from the greater number of different types of people, the freer our democratic society will be, the richer and more unpredictable our art.

Humanists know that something has gone wrong in the academy itself, as it reflects this multi-media world: the atomization of the curriculum; the mindless response to career education or to ethnic chauvinism; the race after students at any educational price; the "training" of the "professional" actor or musician rather than the education of the sympathetic amateur; the frantic search for funds to support the university. In all of these, higher education has often capitulated to the vulgar side of public relations and journalism, selling itself to the highest bidder. Still, the students have grown up in a world of mass communications and are naturally attracted to it; still, teachers of literature themselves now spend as much time watching television and reading newspapers or magazines and listening to the radio as reading books. Inevitably, the most vibrant people—students and teachers alike—are highly selective in their use of the media, and this is the ideal attitude of mind for every humanist to develop in his classes; but the impact for most of us is very profound indeed. It is clear that if the study of the humanities is to have a more vital future, it must appropriate mass communications as a humanistic discipline and not treat it as only popular culture or assign it to another program, institute, or school of professional education. And from this awareness comes my ninth lesson: the essential connection that needs to be made between the liberal arts and mass communications.

IX

In the past few years, with the enormous growth of mass communications as a field of study in American colleges, the primary question asked of anyone implementing a program has centered upon the number of jobs available in the field or the amount of equipment necessary. Practicing professionals have, for the most part, taught the subject. But communications should be a course of study as important to a young person's education as sociology or political science or foreign languages and should be integrated into the liberal arts curriculum. One does not justify the study of literature, history, or philosophy in terms of careers; one should not defend communications only on grounds of its popular appeal or the number of jobs available. One must understand its sociology and history and technology and art and literature because it is the subject of our time and of the future. No lawyer or doctor or teacher can function well without a liberal arts education, and communications must be fundamental to that education.

Like many subjects in the liberal arts curriculum, communications will be broadly interdisciplinary, insisting upon the developed skills of writing and speech, and including elements of law, political science, ethics, sociology, psychology, and technology—indeed, every subject in the curriculum as it relates to a popular audience or to public policy. In the past, journalists have had their best training in a broad liberal arts education, with specialization in a traditional academic subject like English or history, and a minor in journalistic subjects like copyediting, an introduction to the media, public relations, and broadcasting. This approach still makes some sense, but mass communications have so thoroughly saturated American life that a unified approach to the field is in order and will provide another strong element in a synthesis for the humanities. Those who have an intense interest will become practitioners, continuing their education at a practically oriented graduate school like the Columbia School of Journalism or a more theoretically oriented institution like the Annenberg School of Communications at the University of Pennsylvania. But the undergraduate curriculum of all students should include courses in data literacy, public policy, economics, graphics, music, history, sociology, speech, English—an amalgam that will strengthen the student's preparation for professional work in mass communications at the same time as it sensitizes him to one of the fundamental purposes of a college education—critical interpretation.[14]

Mass communications can no longer be viewed as

[14] The kind of program I have described is outlined in Appendix 3.

merely an aspect of public policy, a means to an end, a process. Its influence is pervasive, and its connection with the humanities must be organic. Journalism has a rich and varied literary past—not only in the works of Addison and Steele, George Orwell, Mark Twain, Ernest Hemingway, and dozens of other literary figures, but also in the commentary of writers like Milton, who, speaking of censorship and ethical concerns in *Areopagitica,* sends us back to the great texts and involves us centrally in literature, history, and philosophy. Television, photography, photojournalism are visual media that will be seen only superficially if the student lacks the perspective that great art provides: the same can be said of other disciplines in the humanities and social sciences. Practitioners in book publishing, advertising, public relations, and journalism must have an enormous fund of information and need to develop critical skills that force them to call into question their own work in mass communications.

The future of humanistic thought depends upon a sensible articulation between the complex conditions of modern communications and their historical or ethical dimensions. The phenomenal popularity of *Roots*—in book form and in television—is no accident; people do not want to forego their past. The exposure of governmental corruption, in a book like *All the President's Men,* introduces the ethical implications of mass communications and starts people thinking in ways that activate the humanities. We know that the dramatization of a book on stage, film, or television stimulates the reading of the original. We know that the popularity of a book is directly stimulated by its author's appearance on talk shows and that the talk shows in turn use authors to enhance their own interest. It is the special obligation of humanists to make these inevitable connections between the humanities and the broad subject of mass communications so that they humanize students who will soon be running the media. Otherwise, the humanists themselves will simply be cut off from a contemporary culture influenced and essentially taught by those who operate the communications industries.

Once there was an ebb and flow to serious study that comforted all of us who have loved books and had the good fortune to talk about them to students; we taught students who emulated our professional lives. What could be more gratifying? Now we have a far more complex yet equally important task. We need to persuade our students that one cannot be either a practitioner or a viewer of mass communications without the study of this field firmly settled in a liberal arts context. Mass communications must be made a humanistic discipline; then the study of language and literature, illustrated by the greatest literary texts our students can absorb, will have its organic relationship to the one area of public policy that dominates all of our lives. To the degree that we are successful, we will help to shape our world rather than be shaped by it.

X

There was another lesson—my tenth—that developed from the experience of Open Admissions. It centered upon the activity that we in the universities have designated as "creative" writing. When I began to teach, in the late fifties, some of my finest students were motivated to continue the study of literature in graduate schools and became teachers or college professors. Their professional needs determined the curriculum and automatically made them into fledgling literary critics; indeed, I often thought that the subject they encountered was not literature but literary criticism. In the seventies, the students who seemed to have the greatest love of language and literature were those who aggressively wanted to become poets, novelists, and essayists in the manner of Lowell or Mailer or Ellison or Plath. At first, I saw the development of a strong undergraduate program in creative writing, followed by a master's program, as a necessary balance to the heavy presence of basic writing—one needed wine as well as bread in one's academic diet.[15] Soon, however, it became apparent that the students were more interested

[15] There was money in the budgets of the early 1970s, and we were able to hire John Hawkes, Joseph Heller, and Gwendolyn Brooks in one academic year and later Anthony Burgess, Kurt Vonnegut, Donald Barthelme, Francine Gray, Adrienne Rich, Susan Sontag—a gallery of remarkable writers, who remained for a semester or a year and attracted students of all ages. For a time, the program was the finest in the country. All of that is a memory now, but there is an administrative lesson to be learned. A successful program in creative writing, mass communications, or any of the performing arts is one that has a small but strong core staff of full-time faculty and a range of visiting professionals-in-residence who return regularly to the program. It is important for students to work with professional artists, and those artists should be available to see a student through to the completion of his project or training; it is also important for the students to know that full-time faculty anchor the program in a permanent way. For institutions that have economic difficulties, this is one way of reducing tenured lines—it is also, in my view, the most dramatic and direct way of projecting an excitement in the arts.

in writing than in reading, often at the peril of their prospective careers as writers. Instructors of literature complained that the students knew so little literature and the instructors of writing became troubled by the absence of a formal control in language—even when that control was self-consciously violated by dialect or colloquialisms or solecisms. Still there was the irrepressible motivation of creativity through which one could insist upon the necessary reading. As a consequence, we were able to encourage what Emerson has called creative reading, where every thought is challenged and where the act of reading assumes a far more personal purpose and meaning.

The connection between creative writing and reading is direct and obvious. But analogues can and should be made to acting, painting and sculpture, music, film, and dance—fields in which students have shown intense interest and which will provide most of their lifelong exposure to the humanities. Students who engage in a production of *Antigone* should be simultaneously studying Greek civilization with faculty from the classics department; participants in *King Lear* should be engaged in a seminar taught by an interdisciplinary faculty that speaks of old age and the family as well as of Renaissance culture. Each young actor, painter, musician, film maker, or dancer should be drawn into the full cultural context of his performing art; he should not be allowed to concentrate strictly on craft.

The student's fascination with the techniques of acting and painting, the intricacies of film production, the technology of television should be encouraged in every possible way, but it must also be related constantly to the cultural background that gives the creative act its perspective and deepest meaning. We all know that very few students—2 per cent of all performing arts majors, for example—will earn a living from the art form for which they train; in this sense, if no other, programs in the arts must be far more than pre-professional. One of their legitimate claims for support, one of the most important reasons for their existence, is that they will train students to be more sensitive readers, more perceptive viewers of theater, film, television, and dance. More than almost any disciplines in the curriculum, the creative and performing arts prepare students for activities that will dominate their leisure time, which in fact will consume almost all of their time as they live longer and work less. The arts will offer those millions of Americans who live far beyond their working years much more than entertainment; they will provide a lifelong learning of great diversity that, incidentally, will also assure a future for the humanities.

XI

The need for continuing education is the eleventh, the penultimate, lesson that I learned from the experience of Open Admissions.

Too often we see the extension of education beyond graduate school as a separate enterprise for a different kind of student. But the educational process in American cities can no longer be neatly defined as twelve years that take the student to the college door and then four years later send him to the larger door that opens upon the world. The imagery has changed—for all of us. We witness a revolving door that not only brings the student back to college at different moments in his life but that exposes him to so many other forms of education—television is only the most obvious—at the same time as he sits in a formal classroom. In urban colleges, especially, the varying ages of the students compel us to reconsider the connection between the college and the community in terms of lifelong learning. A year ago, an eighty-three-year-old man enrolled in the Creative Writing Program at The City College; a woman in my seminar is the mother of teen-agers; another is a teacher in a high school that sends us its students. The roster reflects so great a variety of people with a range of preparation and background so diverse that the only common quality seems to be motivation. The essential quality—motivation.

Across the country, and especially in urban centers, working people are returning to school—on weekends, in the evenings, and summers, for part-time education or in pursuit of academic degrees. Some want certificated programs in creative writing, fine and performing arts, and communications—coherent programs that are dependent, at least in part, upon the study of philosophy, history, literature, and science. Because they have the money and desire to travel, they want to understand foreign languages; because they see more theater, they are attracted to courses in drama; because they visit museums, they look for guidance in understanding what they see.

The entire shape of higher education is changing dramatically, and private colleges—with the exception of those still able to be selective—that insist upon offering only the liberal arts to students between the ages of eighteen and twenty-two will continue to close their doors. In the last year alone, the student population entering elementary school has diminished by 4 per cent; the projection for the next ten years is 25 per cent. At the same time, the population of people between the ages of twenty and fifty will increase. These figures are significant enough for educators to reconsider the scope and method of their academic offerings. They have a particular urgency when one realizes that the adult population is highly motivated and prepared to continue their education without necessarily earning credits or formal degrees. Doctors, lawyers, architects, businessmen, engineers, teachers, and secretaries want career development in a university context where the teaching is highly professional. We are beginning to witness this tendency in continuing education, and I can see a form of post-professional training only flourish in the years ahead—indeed, in many institutions it will be the dominant form of education.

The greatest audience for the study of the humanities extends even beyond the working population to those retired people who now find entertainment and education in local churches, libraries, and community centers, where adult education has become a way of life during the evenings and on weekends. This audience has grown dramatically as a consequence of early retirement and economic conditions that have caused the work force to shrink. An urban college, with its extensive resources, has an obligation not only to the young and to the currently employed but to the elderly, who await a structure that will allow them to participate in learning.

Although the college should be the geographical center of activity, offering a range of courses leading to formal degrees, alternative certificates, or simply to the experience of the course itself, a satellite form of education will extend the education directly into the community. The fact is that many people—particularly the elderly—who resist regular travel in the evenings would be inclined to take a course in a local library or community center, their nursing or retirement homes, or even in somebody's home. If courses were offered in different areas of the city and led to the possibility of earning a degree; if the faculty were extended to include retired professors as well as practicing professionals in the city, a network of education would be established that could be exciting to a greatly enlarged student body. Administrators and faculty will have to realize that education is not always where the buildings of a college may be but where the faculty is—especially in a time when most adult students are commuters.

The use of television in bringing together rather than separating individual learners also offers enormous possibilities—especially in the performing and fine arts and the study of foreign languages and history. In a course, students may witness drama three times a week, report upon it, and meet weekly at the college to discuss the experience they've shared with other viewers. Television can visualize and strengthen the language of texts these same viewers or students have read for their classwork. Already an experiment at Wayne State University promises a future education complete with degrees for people who cannot be physically present in a classroom in the manner of conventional undergraduates. Members of local unions improve themselves—in the logical extension of Emersonian self-reliance, of Open Admissions—and the education on television as well as the weekly discussions in the classrooms become the subjects for discussion in the local newspapers. This has been the experience at Wayne State; it may be adapted at the City University and elsewhere. Ultimately, television can be a prime force in the future of the humanities—especially in fields like classical culture—if we accept it as another product of the fictive imagination.

For this increased activity in the humanities, faculty will be needed. Many impressive teachers of the humanities have retired from our urban colleges, partially because of an increased work load that prevents them from pursuing their personal scholarship, partially because they have reached mandatory retirement age. They live in the metropolitan community and want to teach courses more closely related to their writing—for the modest compensation any professional expects, but particularly for the continuation of their own active careers as scholars; they too want a form of continued growth. It is, after all, an educational scandal that we lay waste the talents of our elders and an aspect of the dehumanization of our society that we retire people educationally just because we must retire them economically. In the humanities, especially, early retirement is lamentable, for—to use Daniel Bell's terms—the humanities are concentrative rather than sequential (like the sciences) or linked (like the social sciences). One reads for a lifetime and, one hopes, more profoundly with age.

A second source of faculty are the alumni whose professional careers represent almost every aspect of urban life. Some colleges do use their graduates and working colleagues as professionals-in-residence for programs in performing arts, communications, fine arts, and other disciplines. But too many have not begun to take advantage of those in public policy positions who can explore the difficulties of translating ethics and values into the daily decisions that must be made. The ivory tower, in modern education, is another building in another city—another feature of public policy, as vulnerable to fiscal and political crises as any other urban institution. The educational enterprise, which is lifelong, belongs to all of us. Once we realize that fact, in all of its particulars—once we can accept the need for Open Admissions and sophisticated lifelong learning in the same college—we will extend the meaning of the humanities in ways that are essential to our older as well as our younger citizens, to our external as well as to our internal faculty.

The great danger, as always, is that the educational process will become further atomized. Continuing education must not be separated from the central concerns of the campus or be allowed to function with its own faculty and administration and students. It must grow organically from the academic disciplines and be tied to them: the philosophy department must monitor all courses in philosophy, the history department all courses in history, whether they are in resident instruction or in continuing education. If we do not make this essential connection, we will sacrifice the older and more diverse student population to organizations that have no relationship to higher education, that are purely vocational and entrepreneurial—the roadshows of continuing education, as they have been called.

I do not pretend that these recommendations are simple to effect, but I am convinced that they represent a more imaginative future for the humanities than currently exists. In earlier ages, self-selected coteries went to soirées and spoke of literature, philosophy, science, and the arts— of culture, in the broadest sense; it was a form of continuing education, although distant to the larger population. In America, we have democratized higher education for the young, and this creates problems that need to be resolved, especially for the majority of underprepared students, largely through a required curriculum—at least for the first year of their college education. For those who would continue to be educated, we need to create a college that suggests a student is of no prescribed age—that all of us, and especially "teachers," are students. By drawing older people into the educational community, by extending the faculty to include retired professors and professionals-in-residence, by having the classroom in a home or a library or a community center or on television as well as on the campus, the college becomes a center where the humanities may have a far more varied future. It humanizes a culture too polarized between education and entertainment, between vocationalism and liberal arts, between the old and young, the men and the women, the "haves" and the "have-nots." It humanizes its participants, whether they be people who need skills to survive in American society, whether they be professionals who want to remain professionally *au courant*, or whether they wish to continue the education of their imagination.

XII

These are the public lessons I have learned from Open Admissions, and I hope they are of value to other teachers and administrators and students throughout the school systems of America. My outline of a synthesis for the study of the humanities is rooted in the practicalities of our daily lives as educators. Thus, the retraining of teachers and the sequential study of language and literature, of composition and reading, are essential to a future for the humanities, for they give coherence to the discipline; and the use of tutors in summer programs and during the academic year, to aid the classroom teacher, will make the implementation of sequential study far easier.

These are public lessons. A core curriculum at the college level that sets forth clear intentions will give guidance to earlier levels of instruction. And once the student has a firm grasp of his skills as a writer and some acquaintance with the great texts in literature, history, and philosophy, he can then continue to see the humanistic implications in his pre-professional training and make a final synthesis in the kind of capstone seminar dealing with human values that I have described. As he leaves his college, he can anticipate a lifetime of learning that will go far beyond whatever career he pursues, far into his retirement and into the study of subjects he could only touch upon in college: foreign languages and art and theater and music and literature—the humanizing subjects of life that will make his life more humane.

These are, as I say, my public lessons. The final lesson is personal and, therefore, most profound—at least for me.

From the moment I entered Columbia University and embarked upon a professional career in the study of the humanities, the texts I have cherished most have championed freedom of expression—Milton's *Areopagitica*, Emerson's *American Scholar*, Mill's *On Liberty*—and the self-reliance of the simple separate person: *Moby Dick* and *Walden* and *Song of Myself* and *Invisible Man*. Independence. Individualism. All the colleagues and students and friends I have felt closest to in these twenty-five years have carried on this fundamental freedom and have given the humanities the life they deserve at The City College and elsewhere in this country.

When I perceived the problems of Open Admissions, I could have chosen not to write about them. As a senior administrator and full professor with tenure, I was in a most privileged position in American education—one conducive to silence and self-protection. I could have continued to help manage the college, struggling with my colleagues to shape an academic future despite the forces I have described. Or, I could have resigned and written the article and, by withdrawing, sacrificed the opportunity to improve, administratively, our common condition. I would then have placed myself in my present position—a writer whose ideas may or may not be implemented by other administrators. I could have—I could have—but, of course, I could not have: the article and this book are indeed both public and personal acts, and represent, finally, a matter of character.

It all finally does come down to a matter of character. For all of us caught in the search for honest answers that go beyond ourselves. So many forces in this experience of Open Admissions have caused decent people to tear at each other, to be less than civilized to one another. A vast number of underprepared students were brought into a major university equipped to carry on conventional academic programs—and too few people estimated the long-range bill. When that bill came due, year after year, the city and the state refused to pay it—and the faculty hired to do the job were fired, and the administrators who did the firing were assaulted. No wonder people tore at one another. Then the college was fully tenured, with a diminishing number of students, most of whom needed training in basic skills before they could study college subjects. Then the construction of necessary buildings was delayed so that the physical conditions grew quite unbearable. And every effort in curriculum design or academic planning seemed impaled upon the next decreasing budget projection. The conscientious faculty concentrated upon their individual courses—no larger future seemed available—while the disenchanted and disgruntled said, "So what," and no one spoke of faculty morale any longer. There was none. Finally, taxpayers and their legislative representatives said, "No, we will not give more money to educational institutions that do not prepare students adequately for colleges or jobs—that do not produce a literate citizenry. More money has not solved the problems spawned by illiteracy. You educators must set your own house in order, within the ample budget we have given you. If your student needs do not match your faculty competencies, that is your business. And tenure is your business. Here is your budget—no more." And here we are, educators in the center of an urban society, trapped in a history that has produced conventional scholar/teachers and a new generation of students, many of whom are underprepared, the largest number of students seeking a college education the world has ever known—our collective American future.

It would be too easy to cast a stone. Obviously, there should have been far more careful planning and a massive commitment to underprepared students before they entered college if all of us—politicians, minorities, and educators together—really wanted Open Admissions to be successful. Certainly, we should have made a distinction between the students who could master those skills necessary for work in a community college and those who could deal with the subject matter of a senior college.

It would be so easy to cast a stone. But simplistic judgment would be a distortion, too, for out of these ashes something like a phoenix has arisen—good work has been accomplished, after all, and its effects will be seen in years to come. The leaders of Open Admissions—from the chancellor and his staff to the individual presidents and their associates—were, for the most part, decent people, highly competent, always pressured, victims of political forces over which they had little control, struggling to achieve excellence and accommodation at the same time, and succeeding in many ways that will one day become clearer. At The City College, ·where poor students will continue to climb the streets toward that academic city upon a hill and raise their eyes from the cracked pavement of their lives, a new theater now serves a whole community, within and without the college; programs accommodate future doctors and lawyers and architects and engineers and nurses; a faculty of decent people educate, despite all of the problems I have described, the ill-prepared as well as the more fortunate, and are struggling to balance Open Admissions and academic excellence in the same institution.

If there is one last personal lesson in this experience of Open Admissions, it is the absolute necessity for educators to fight for their independence as educators. What happened to me had everything to do with political pressures and nothing to do with education. Independence is what we have lost—and with it almost our profession—and that is what needs to be regained. In the sixties, too many of us surrendered fundamental humanistic beliefs to the evanescence of student demands, community and political pressures—we sought the love of students and of the community and lost, soon after, their respect. In the seventies we confronted legislators who too often insisted upon nothing but accountability and converted so many who should have been intellectual and moral and social leaders into the accountants of higher education.

A future for the humanities must lie in our hands. We need to shape the future on our own terms, without sacrificing sensitivity to the demands of students and local communities, minorities and the aged, and bearing in mind that Open Admissions can embody the essential truth expressed in Dewey's belief that democracy is "primarily a mode of associated living, of conjoint communicated experience," one that can break down "those barriers of class, race, and national territory" which have kept men and women "from perceiving the full import of their activity." At the same time, and in the same university, we must so discipline ourselves—our internal budgets, our academic planning—that no single political pressure group will steal away our independence. Our autonomy has been lost because we have reacted to social conditions instead of anticipating them and not always spoken with the cogency that comes from a deep belief in the value of the humanities. Our actions have been dictated by forces brought upon us—student protests, Open Admissions, the insurgent demands of minorities and women, the taxpayers' demand for accountability. Education need not be entirely reactive. On our terms, we must create universities of Open Admissions and academic excellence: it is the only way they will be created. If we sacrifice either objective, we sacrifice ourselves as educators. I know that what I am asking is extraordinarily difficult to achieve, but we have no choice. And we have the lessons of these years, at the City University of New York, from which all of us, in the cities of this country, can learn.

APPENDIX 1

A Budget Projection for a Writing Program

The Teacher Fellowships

There are three fundamental objectives to the teacher-fellowship program:

(1) To improve instruction in writing and reading in the participating schools by involving key teachers in the development of sequential writing and reading programs.

(2) To make available to the participating teachers, and through them to other teachers in their schools, summaries of what is being done in the areas of reading and writing instruction.

(3) To publish and distribute widely the curricular materials developed for each grade level in the program. In time, a series of graded texts in writing, growing out of the fellowship program, will be published by the National Center for Literacy.

This budget projection does not include the detailed items—fringe benefits to participating faculty, overhead, etc.—that one normally includes in a full presentation; the final estimate would therefore be somewhat higher. The following is simply a rough estimate of what a fellowship program would entail.

THE TEACHER-FELLOWSHIP PROGRAM (Cluster of 15)

12 teachers @ $3,500 per year	$42,000.00
(Spring seminar @ $750; summer teaching @ $2,000; fall seminar @ $750)	
2 co-ordinators @ $4,000 per year:	8,000.00
(Spring seminar @ $1,000; summer teaching @ $2,000; fall seminar @ $1,000)	
1 evaluator @ $3,500 per year	3,500.00
	$53,500.00

A Summer Writing Camp

The summer writing workshop has three purposes:

(1) To improve the writing and reading skills of students who enroll in the workshop.

(2) To motivate students to develop language skills early in their educational experience as a means of improving the quality of academic work, lowering the dropout rate, especially of students in the high schools and colleges, and reducing the cost of remediation of higher school levels.

(3) To provide a laboratory of significant size for testing and evaluating in an actual classroom situation the fourteen-year sequential curriculum in writing which the teacher-fellowship program aims to create.

The budget projection for 350 students—25 students from each of the twelve grades in the participating schools as well as 50 students recruited for the two college workshops—would break down as follows:

A SUMMER WRITING WORKSHOP (350 students)

20 *tutors* @ $500 per summer: Each tutor with 17–18 students, in 4 groups of 4–5 each, 16 hours a week = 120 hours a summer @ $4.00 = $500 a tutor x 20 tutors[1]	$10,000.00
1 *laboratory proctor:* 120 hours @ $4.00 = $500	500.00

1 secretarial assistant: 165 hours @ $3.00	500.00
1 evaluator:	1,000.00
Teaching materials:	2,000.00
Daily newspapers and teaching materials for 350 students for 4 days a week x 8 weeks	
	$14,000.00

[1] I have rounded out all estimates.

APPENDIX 2

A National Center for Literacy

A National Center for Literacy should have three units: the Research Unit on Literacy, the Conference Unit on Literacy, and the Projects Unit on Literacy.

The Research Unit on Literacy, although national in reference, will serve regional and local projects. It will gather, publish, and disseminate data on research and instruction in literacy. It will make available to teachers in a participating school knowledge of what has been done and of what is being done to develop more effective ways to teach students how to read and write. It will be responsible for establishing evaluation designs for all projects implemented by the Projects Unit on Literacy. It will award fellowships for the development of pragmatic projects to help improve the language skills of Americans. These projects will be approved by a Director of Research and the director's staff. Finally, the Research Unit will recommend these pragmatic projects for examination by participants—experts in the field—who will be invited to the conferences, seminars, and workshops sponsored by the Conference Unit.

The Conference Unit on Literacy will invite participants from across the nation to examine the pragmatic projects recommended by the Research Unit. The scope of the project will determine the length of the seminar or workshop. A workshop may be as short as one day or as long as eight weeks. This external and second-stage screening of a project will give donors the complete consultation normally required before funding.

The Projects Unit on Literacy will design and direct the practical programs to improve reading, writing, and listening skills. It will also be responsible for funding. Projects will have regional and local orientation, although export versions of successful projects may be adapted to the needs of other parts of the country. It is expected that local corporations and businesses will fund local projects of the National Center for Literacy. The City Writing Projects —the teacher-fellowship program and the summer writing camp— are two projects designed especially for teachers and students in New York City. Clearly they will be exportable to all cities with similar problems. They call for a co-operative effort by a city college, a public school system, and the corporate interests of the city. Many other projects can be implemented through a National Center for Literacy:

1. The use of daily newspapers in the teaching of reading and writing.

2. The development of television programming in the teaching of literacy skills.

3. The planning of literacy programs for business, industry, and special groups.

4. The use of television and print advertising to persuade audiences that reading and writing are a source of pleasure.

5. A book campaign to get attractive books into the hands of children, particularly in poverty areas where books are an unattainable luxury.

6. The development of public library facilities and programs for young and adult readers and the publication of large print books for the old.

7. The rewriting of texts, insurance policies, legal documents, medical information, and consumer information for easier communication.

8. The publication of bilingual interlinear newspapers and newsletters as a means of language instruction.

9. The integration of career-oriented programs and the teaching of literacy skills.

10. The teaching of typing in the lower grades to motivate the development of literacy skills.

11. The use of translation projects for young students, as they move from a native language to English as a second language.

APPENDIX 3

A Program in Mass Communications

The following is an outline for a program in communications that attempts to integrate the study of journalism and broadcasting with traditional academic disciplines. As one model, it suggests the beginning of an organic program in mass communications.

Curriculum

Majors in communications will be expected to fulfill the following requirements: a *general academic core* of 38 credits common to all students in the College of Liberal Arts and Science; a *communications component* of 16 credits; a *public policy component* of 12 credits; *professional specialization* in print and electronic journalism, 12 credits, or broadcasting, 10 to 11 credits; a *work-study internship and seminar*, 8 credits; *electives*, 42–44 credits. It is desirable that 16 of these elective credits be in a single field of special interest.

I. *Fundamentals of Communications* (16 credits)
Students will be required to take
    English: Writing Workshop in Prose (4)
    Speech: Communications through Speech (4)
    Art: The Visual Arts as Communication (4)
and *one* of the following three courses:

English: The Mass Media and Society (4)
Political Science: Mass Media and Politics (4)
Sociology: Theory of Mass Culture and Mass Communications (4)

II. *Fundamentals of Public Policy* (12 credits)
Political Science: Introduction to Public Policy (4)
Economics: Public Finance (4)
Political Science: Introduction to Quantitative Data Literacy

III. *Communications Specialization* (10–12 credits)
Students will be required to specialize in *one* of the following two areas:

1. *Print and Electronic Journalism* (take 4 of 5 courses):
English: Journalistic Writing (3)
English: Feature Article Writing (3)
English: Copy Editing (3)
English: Broadcast Journalism (3)
English: Public Relations (3)

2. *Broadcasting* (take 3 of 4 courses):
Speech: Foundations of Broadcasting (3)
Speech: Radio-television Production (4)
Speech: Broadcast Documentary (4)
English: Broadcast Journalism (3)

IV. *Internship* (8 credits)
Students in their senior year will be placed in jobs in mass media firms, agencies, and institutions. The year-long work-study program will also feature regular seminars, under the direction of one or more mentors, to allow students an opportunity to focus on common academic concerns and to share ideas and insights obtained through individual work-study programs. Students will earn credit through the following courses:
English: Co-operative Education (3) (2 semesters)
English: Group Tutorial (1) (2 semesters)

V. *Free Electives* (42–44 credits)
Students are advised to take a sequence of 16 credits in an aca-

demic specialization of their interest as part of their free electives. Such a choice should be in some field outside the communications component that would lend perspective to and be of significance in the broad context of their work.

ACKNOWLEDGMENTS

In the midst of the events described in these pages, I often thought of my life as a design of human circles that grew smaller and smaller until they reached, in Emerson's words, the first circle—my own eye, my own self.

On the outer orb lived all the people in my profession of education, the many readers of *Saturday Review,* those City College alumni who wrote me hundreds of encouraging letters. Thanks to these people who cared enough to write. Thanks also to Joel Colton and Lydia Bronte of the Rockefeller Foundation for their personal support and to the foundation itself for a grant that allowed me time to complete this book. Loretta Barrett has been an extremely sensitive and perceptive editor, reminding me constantly of how the problems of The City College reflect those of colleges throughout America.

At and near my college, dozens of good friends called when it was so important to call—Elie and Marion Wiesel, Earl Ubell, Edward Quinn, Mina Shaughnessy, M. L. Rosenthal, Martin and Nancy Delman, Dennis DeNitto, Harold and Norman Levine, Louise Roberts, and many, many others among the faculty and students of The City College. I wish to thank them all. Saul Brody, who was witness to this academic drama and never flinched in his support, was the associate every dean deserves to have; he was also a sensitive reader of my manuscript in its various stages. To my secretary, Ruth Rosenzweig, thanks for making the dailiness of my existence during this time more bearable. Still others reminded me of how lucky I have been to know so many decent human beings—Arthur Waldhorn, Arthur Zeiger, Edmund Volpe, Leo Hamalian, and Benjamin DeMott. Thanks to them for their friendship and for having read part or all of my manuscript before it became my book.

In that closer circle of my family, I am most grateful to my brother and sister-in-law, Gene and Sonja, who never left the telephone when the crisis was most crushing and who made important suggestions for revisions in the manuscript. To my good mother, who gasped at *Newsweek* and naturally thought her son had aged twenty years because of all this—to my mother, thanks, and to my father, also, gone now nineteen years but alive in my mind and heart as the shaping power of my conscience: thanks to my parents for all their unremembered acts of kindness and of love. To my children, Donna and Jonathan, who laughed when I was morbidly serious and grew serious when I pretended not to care—thanks; without them all of this would have been distorted, like a life without a family. And finally, at the center, at the heart, where no one else lives, thanks to my remarkable wife—to Selma, thanks, for having read this manuscript so many times but, more importantly, for having been there always, all the time. She never asked for this trial. But when it came she never ceased to give and sympathize and control. Thanks:

> *Thanks to the human heart by which we live*
> *Thanks to its tenderness, its joys, and fears,*
> *To me the meanest flower that blows can give*
> *Thoughts that do often lie too deep for tears.*

INDEX

U49